Dedication

To women bodybuilders all over the world — and especially to those fantastic girls who competed in the Miss Olympia contest who helped make this book possible.

Special thanks to Maria Shriver who helped so much with the publicity and promotion of our Miss Olympia contest.

1980 Miss Olympia place winners: Left to right-Stacey Bentley, 5th place; Corrine Machado, 4th place; Rachel McLish, 1st place; Lynn Conkwright, 3rd place; and Auby Paulick, 2nd place.

Rachel McLish, Miss Olympia 1980 and George Snyder.

WOMEN OF THE OLYMPIA

THE PHENOMENON OF WOMEN'S BODYBUILDING

by
George Snyder and Rick Wayne

RUNNING PRESS
PHILADELPHIA, PENNSYLVANIA

Copyright © 1981 by Olympus Health & Recreation Inc.
All rights reserved under the Pan-American and International
Copyright Conventions. Printed in the United States of America.

9   8   7   6   5   4   3   2   1
Digit on the right indicates the number of this printing.

Canadian representatives: John Wiley & Sons Canada, Ltd.
22 Worcester Road, Rexdale, Ontario M9W 1L1

International representatives: Kaiman & Polon, Inc.
2175 Lemoine Avenue, Fort Lee, New Jersey 07024

Library of Congress Cataloging in Publication Data

Snyder, George.
  Women of the Olympia.

  1. Bodybuilding for women. I. Wayne, Rick, 1938–
II. Title.
GV546.6.W64S68   646.7′5   81-10696
ISBN 0-89471-139-3 (pbk.)
ISBN 0-89471-140-7 (lib. bdg.)

The authors are grateful for the use of photos by
John Balik, Craig Deitz, John Campos, Bob Long
and Rich Ruoti.

This book may be ordered directly from the publisher.
Please include 75 cents postage.

Try your bookstore first.

RUNNING PRESS
125 South Twenty-Second Street
Philadelphia, Pennsylvania 19103

CONTENTS

IN THE BEGINNING
HOW IT ALL STARTED
THE MAKEUP OF A COMPETITOR
THE MISS OLYMPIA CONTEST
HOW THEY TOOK IT
WHAT THEY SAID
A NEW DIRECTION
THE CHOICE IS YOURS
PLANNING YOUR TRAINING ROUTINE

Suzy Green dazzles the audience in Philadelphia at the Miss Olympia contest in 1980.

Rachel McLish wins the 1980 Miss Olympia and is flanked by (left) publisher Joe Weider and (right) Ben Weider, president of the International Federation of Bodybuilders. Center, Dyna-Cam executive Lloyd Lambert who sponsored the contest.

In The Beginning

IT is not at all easy facing up to the at times embarrassing fact that a new sport called female bodybuilding has caught most of us with our pants somewhere around our ankles. The signals were all around us for a long time but we were so blinded by conventional prejudices we never saw the ominous writing on the wall until it was too . . . well, let us say until quite recently. Now that female bodybuilding has busted clear of its embryonic cocoon to hog prime time on national television, now that the strangely put together moth is out in the open, bold as brass and making regular ostentatious landings on the pages of our more prestigious newspapers and magazines, a tidal wave of concern is rising among members of the medical profession and the once male dominated world of bodyweights and measurements, particularly among the proprietors of health studios throughout the country.

Rachel McLish and Miss Olympia runner-up Auby Paulick treat cameramen to another look at their prizewinning legs.

Lorie Johnston (left to right) Rachel, Suzy Green and Patsy Chapman await results of the 1980 Miss Olympia contest. One year earlier Patsy had been declared winner of the Best In The World award.

For by their well-attended public exhibitions around the nation the new wave female bodybuilders have sparked off explosive discussions everywhere, much of the ensuing controversy centered on what appears to be an inexplicable determination to conquer and hold areas of bodybuilding and weightlifting previously considered the sacred domain of the male by virtue of his more appropriately structured physique.

It seems that the new wave female bodybuilder, whose unusually muscular biceps, abdominals and deltoids shame Charles Atlas, has taken the Women's Lib anything-a-man-can-do-I-can-do war cry way past the job market. Indeed, a leading bodybuilding magazine recently prophesied that it won't be long before the female bodybuilder moves in on the Mr. America title. "Certainly, the move will not suffer from a lack of muscle on the part of the women," the magazine noted in its editorial.

Truth is that, by their physical appearance, many of the new wave female bodybuilders are adding fuel to the growing suspicion that unless they are discouraged, unless their sport is given new direction, the female body as it has been known and admired by conventional men and women since the beginning of time might be in

Corrine Machado, Auby Paulick, Lynn Conkwright and Rachel McLish took fourth, second, third and first places respectively in the Miss Olympia. It had been close between Rachel and Auby.

danger of being replaced by a monstrosity, an aberration, if you will, synonymous with over-developed muscles and the absence of all that once identified a human form as female.

The leading champions of the new sport nearly all display abnormally flat, though extremely muscular, chests and pancake derrieres. There is precious little about their reformed physiques to differentiate them from their male counterparts. Their bodies have been stripped so clean of fat the better to display their unusual muscularity, that where sensuous valleys and attractive curves once played havoc with the male libido nothing exists now but flat terrain . . . in all its sinewy detail.

Even the postures that female bodybuilders adopt onstage, and by which they are judged at contests, are not dissimilar from those made famous by Steve Reeves and John Grimek in their Mr. America heyday and by current number one male bodybuilder Arnold Schwarzenegger.

Which is not to say female bodybuilding is without support. On the contrary, the muscular women of the sport currently enjoy a popularity on par with some of the nation's top rock shows. Where once their presence onstage

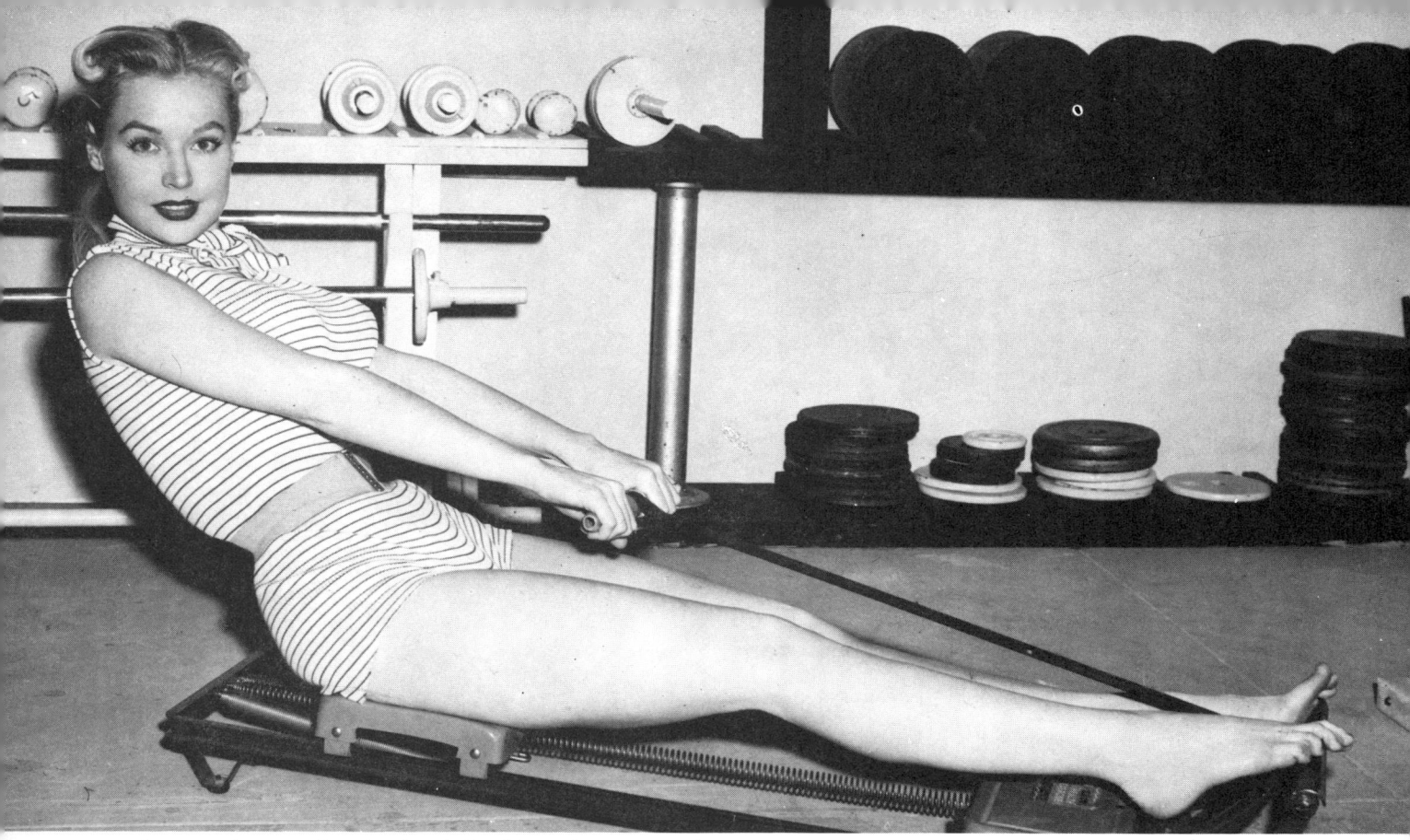

Betty Weider, wife of publisher Joe Weider, still retains the looks and shape that made her a leading covergirl.

was frowned upon by the bodybuilders fraternity the new wave female bodybuilders are now stars in their own right. Why? As one well known male physique champion put it, "What circus worthy of its name is without a fat lady?" And that is what concerns bodybuilding promoters most. For years they fought to create a good image for their sport. Time and time again they preached about the wondrous effect of weight-training on the male and female body. Bodybuilding with weights was the best way to develop muscular body mass, symmetry and power, said the advertisements to diffident young males everywhere. Weight-training did not turn a man into a muscle bound freak incapable of combing his own hair.

Sometimes the advertisers pointed to beautifully shaped ladies who had ostensibly trimmed and firmed their figures through weight-training. Weights have a different effect on the female body, shouted the advertisements from bodybuilding magazines. Women were, well, *different*. They did not have what it takes to build large and muscular bodies. Exercising with weights could only give them *curvaceous* and firm figures . . . like Betty Weider's. Betty, who as Miss Brosmer was everything the healthy, well-built and strong American male ever dreamed about. There were the pictures of Jayne Mansfield perched on the muscular shoulders of her Mr. Universe husband Mikey Hargitay and the captions that quoted the lady as saying she owed everything to exercising with barbells and dumbbells.

April Nicotra was a big winner until she entered the Miss Olympia contest and was floored by the new criteria. Here she receives congratulations on winning the Miss Eastern United States title from Arnold Schwarzenegger and George Snyder.

Of course, the advertisements were not sufficient to convince all women that they could exercise with weights and still not develop muscle like Steve Reeves and Mickey Hargitay. So the magazines hired writers to explain why it was nigh impossible for females to build dense muscle that showed through their skin. Much of their explanations centered on some supposed difference between male and female chromosomes. For those were the days before it became common knowledge that "women lack the androgen receptors neccessary for protein synthesis and muscle hypertrophy." Before everyone knew men have "a greater range of both slow-twitch and fast twitch muscle fibres."

The campaign to convince women that they could, by training with weights three times a week, develop figures comparable to some of Hollywood's leading female stars worked. In America, Jack LaLanne and Vic Tanny would become household names. Millions of women put their overweight selves in the hands of those two and lost excess fat, if also a little weight from their pocketbooks. Bodybuilding became respectable. Normal people were

Joe Weider and Rachel McLish strike another pose for the television cameras.

The muscularity displayed here by contenders for the Miss Olympia title during pre-judging shocked many who were accustomed to a different type of female bodybuilder.

Denmark's Anniqua Fors failed to place in the 1980 Miss Olympia. Not nearly muscular enough, said one judge. Anniqua promised to return for another crack at the title.

saying via endorsements on television and in the print medium that working out with weights had given them a new lease on life, that they had never felt better and, holy toledo, they still were able to comb their own hair without assistance.

The bodybuilding contests that included women never really took off in America, Not for some time anyway. Oh, sure, there were the events that the International Federation of Bodybuilders somewhat reluctantly staged in New York but those were always put on somewhere between the Mr. America and Mr. Universe events, more for comic relief than anything else. The women who participated in events like the Miss Americana, for instance were not the best examples of feminine pulchritude, to use a high-falutin word. And you would never know, judging by their physiques, that ther trained with weights. Indeed, most of them were strippers that desperate scouts had talked into appearing in the aforementioned contest on the ground that here was a great opportunity to advertise their particular talents. These women clearly had no idea what to do once they had been introduced onstage. They came on with bumps and grinds, threw their rearends and other protuberances in the collective face of their audience, kicked up a leg and were off into

Miss Olympia contenders line up for pre-judging.

the wings. Most of the time the orchestra played *The Stripper* as the contestants for the Miss Americana title cavorted on stage, And when each person had presented her act the mostly male audience whistled and screamed for more. There was no need for intermissions in those early days of bodybuilding productions.

On the West Coast a former Mr. Universe named Reg Lewis presented an annual affair that also included girls. Say it straight, Reg had perhaps the best females ever to strut their stuff before a bodybuilding audience. Most of the girls were downright goodlooking, healthy in appearance and always tanned. They were in every way different from the male bodybuilders. They used no oil on their skin, at least not so much that it was obvious. And their poses reminded more of the Miss America pageant *than* a muscle show. And the California fans always gave them a rousing ovation. It came as no surprise later that Reg's girls all came from a *model* agency. Oh, they were cute.

Over in England, however, it was altogether a different story. Already famous for staging the most prestigious of bodybuilding contests, the Mr. Universe, the National Amateur British Bodybuilders Association, took to

Female bodybuilding will receive as much media attention as male bodybuilding, Joe Weider promised audience at Philadelphia Sheraton, venue of 1980 Miss Olympia. Arnold Schwarzenegger, Franco Columbu, and George Snyder were there to back Weider up.

presenting girl bodybuilders with its Mr. Britain contenders and added still another niche to its gun butt. The girls who competed yearly for the Miss Britain title were all seasoned bodybuilders who trained at least three times a week with weights and watched their diets as carefully as their male counterparts.

Those who rose to success in the Miss Britain event were invited to participate in the Miss Bikini contest that the association staged annually with the Mr. Universe show. Truly, the girls of Nabba became famous. Many competed around the holiday resorts of Europe, won, and spread the good word for weight-training. One or two former Miss Britain winners went on to become Miss World.

It must be said that whereas these girls displayed very firm bodies they nevertheless retained all the attributes for which the better endowed female is admired. They showed their figures onstage in a very classy fashion, a little bit of tease here, some raunch there and curves that were nonetheless firm. Many were models in their spare time.

The English picture reproduced itself all over Europe and whereas the American attempt carried a certain disfiguring scar on its face, female bodybuilding on the European scene seemed to do everything to enhance weight-training for the ladies. No wonder American promoters scratched their heads worrying how to emulate the work of Nabba.

Wonderful proof that bodybuilding with weights need not produce the sort of muscularity normally associated with displays by male physique champions. Lorie Johnston is set to go places.

The Miss America pageant was clearly not the way to go. Here it was clear that a competitor's figure was the very least consideration. That would not do. For a while it seemed that bodybuilding, competitive bodybuilding, at any rate, would remain a man's sport. The standard of contender who participated in America's Miss events seemed to dip with each succeeding show. And then those of us with our noses and ears closest to the bodybuilding turf, that is to say, California bodybuilding, began to hear the rumors. Women were working out at Gold's Gym, in Santa Monica, that bastion of male bodybuilding. There was talk about women who trained along with the men, as partners. And some rumors suggested these bold ladies actually shared the gym's locker-room and its showers with their training buddies.

Naturally, we ignored the clearly bizarre reports. And then came *Pumping Iron*, the book. More evidence that females had infiltrated Gold's. In time we saw for ourselves that women were actually hoisting heavy iron with the guys at the aforementioned famous gym and when we talked with these ladies they let us know in no uncertain terms that real bodybuilding was not the pantyhose stuff put out by Jack LaLanne but the very thing we had come to look upon as ours exclusively.

Rachel McLish was guest on "AM-Philadelphia" show shortly before her appearance in the Miss Olympia.

Miss Olympia judges had a difficult time choosing between Rachel McLish and the muscular Auby Paulick (above).

We merely smiled even when we noticed some of the leading exponents of female bodybuilding squatting beneath weights that would give some of us pause. There were girls at Gold's who performed barbell curls with weights comparable to those used by some Mr. America hopefuls.

After a time we got used to the idea of training alongside the women, subconsciously hoping it was all a passing phase, that their participation might well increase the bodybuilding population.

Never once did we see this development leading to a major controversy with the potential to set bodybuilding back years. Not even when Lisa Lyon visited the writer at the offices of Muscle Builder magazine. I was the editor-in-chief of the journal and Lisa had hoped to talk me into featuring the fledgling sport of female bodybuilding. Yes, that's how far they had come in a few months. They had decided on a sport all their own. They were no longer prepared merely to be comic relief at Mr. America promotions.

Female bodybuilders insist on being treated in the same manner accorded their male colleagues. Minutes before appearing onstage, Stacey Bentley, Carolyn Cheshire, and Suzy Green give themselves a last once-over under the experienced eyes of Mike Mentzer, left, and Danny Padilla.

Lisa as she stood in running shorts, tank top and Adidas shoes was an attractive enough bundle. She appeared much more muscular than your average five-foot-nothing female, true, but there was nothing about her that might be interpreted as male. Lisa had the physical appearance of a trained female gymnast, with an eagle sharpness in her eyes that spoke volumes for good health habits. Ah, but then she decided to show me a set of photographs taken of her some weeks earlier. The first ten or so showed her in ballet postures, displayed feminine but unusually muscular thighs, and arms that appeared strong, to say the least. Hey, but in no way unattractive.

And then I came across that photograph with Lisa doing the famous crab pose, the one bodybuilders refer to as "the most muscular". Cripes! For a moment I could not believe this was the same model in the earlier pictures. There were striations across the area which previously had been a firm bustline. Yes, indeed, there was everything men strived for in their pectoral development routines. The chick was ripped as we say. Across the chest, the triceps and the shoulders.

A section of the crowd that packed the Philadelphia Sheraton's ballroom, where the Miss Olympia show was held. Patrons were treated to special dinner in advance of the contest.

I remember asking Lisa to leave her pictures with me, which she reluctantly agreed to do. She told me before leaving that she had done some ballet but her big wish was to see female bodybuilding established along the lines of male bodybuilding. That is to say, Lisa wanted respect for her sister bodybuilders. She said she hoped to see contests organized for female bodybuilders, who were quite something apart from the Jack LaLanne types. "We work out with heavy weights," she pointed out, "We diet and we are every bit as serious about the sport as is the male contender. There is no reason why the muscle magazines should not feature us with the same respect afforded male bodybuilders."

For days afterwards I thought of what Lisa had said to me. I showed her pictures around the office and all of the girls at Weider expressed disgust at the sight of a woman with muscles. They said Lisa was grotesque.

I pointed out that in clothes Lisa was a very attractive female, hinting along the way that she appeared a lot more feminine than some of the self-professed sex-machines behind Weider's typewriters. But I still had not come to terms with the idea af women hitting most muscular poses that showed more triceps and trapezius definition than Lou Ferrigno.

Rick Wayne (left to right), Arnold Schwarzenegger, Betty Weider, George and Margaret Snyder discuss methods of training used by female bodybuilders, during an exhibition at the Sheraton one day after the Miss Olympia.

I learned that Lisa trained with Pete Grymkowski at Gold's and that she had acquired a manager. Clearly this little lady was serious. Unfortunately, I left Weider soon after my meeting with Lisa Lyon and never got around to doing the feature on female bodybuilding that I had promised her I would write.

The next I learned of Lisa Lyon she had become a bodybuilding star. Hardly 14 months since our first meeting Lisa had spearheaded The Bodybuilding Movement by becoming a champion in her own right. The magazines were full of praise for this muscular lady and featured page after page of her hopes for her sport.

Interesting enough, even the newspapers featured Lisa without sarcasm. I received a newspaper clipping from friends in Britain and there was Lisa Lyon, a winner, talking about the leaps that female bodybuilding was making in America.

Still I was not sure I liked what I saw. There was one particular picture of Lisa, that shows her sitting on the floor next to an Olympic barberll, that oozed sex appeal. No grotesque muscle there. I looked and I looked and gradually I began to think that perhaps the fault was in the mind of the beholder, that perhaps I was looking at things with prejudiced eyes, in much the same way that ordinary people looked at male bodybuilding before the advent of *Pumping Iron* and Schwarzenegger. I began to accept Lisa and her sport.

I was not quite ready for what was to come.

Secretary of IFBB Women's Committee, Cathy Gelfo, during a discussion with promoter George Snyder (left) and IFBB president Ben Weider. Cathy helped set up the rules for female contests.

How It All Started

George Snyder had been three times the promoter of bodybuilding contests for women before he was convinced something had to be done if the sport was to approach the status of male physique competition.

He had produced the Miss Eastern United States and in the process discovered that there was no organized body behind female bodybuilding: You put advertisement in some muscle magazine, you offered trophies of some small monetary prize and somewhere in your normal male bodybuilding programme you fitted a woman's contest. A sad state of affairs, Snyder thought.

George had long been a bodybuilding fanatic. Indeed, even as he had watched the Miss Americana on one or two occasions in New York he had felt some compassion for the bodybuilding girls, women who took the sport seriously but were forced, due to circumstances beyond their control, to appear onstage against other women whose main purpose in life had nothing whatever to do with bodybuilding.

Husband and wife team Boyer and Valerie Coe put on a posing exhibition for Miss Olympia audience. Boyer has won numerous physique titles while Valerie helped judge the Miss Olympia contest.

It seemed to George that unless something was done for the female bodybuilders more and more women would lose interest in bodybuilding as a competitive sport. His many discussions with other promoters led to nothing that might have changed the situation for female bodybuilders.

The International Federation of Bodybuilders had established itself as the number one bodybuilding organization in the world but even there it seemed the main effort was to put male bodybuilding on the map. Indeed, under its president Ben Weider, the IFBB had done wonders for the sport. If only something could be done for the women bodybuilders along the lines of Ben Weider's work for the male, Snyder surmised, what a good day for bodybuilding generally this would be. On the other hand it seemed to Snyder that Ben Weider had his hands full with the IFBB. So Snyder hit on the idea of creating his Women Bodybuilder's Association (WBA). There were long discussions with Ben Weider and soon after the formation of the group Snyder applied to the IFBB for affiliation and was readily accepted.

Ben Weider made just one stipulation. George was to make certain that the women who competed in events sponsored by the WBA all trained with weights. Clearly

the plan was to spread the good word on female bodybuilding by offering the best developed figures in America as proof of the wonder of exercising with barbells and dumbbells.

Previously George Snyder had merely put an advertisement in *Muscle Builder* magazine whenever he was staging a contest for female bodybuilders. The girls wrote back to say they planned to compete and on the day of the event they showed up at the venue to be judged. Simple as that. And sometimes there were ladies onstage who had no right in a contest for beautifully developed bodies. With the advent of the WBA, however, contenders now had to apply for inclusion in Snyder's promotions. They were requested to send a recent photograph with the application and, if accepted, were expected to perform certain exercises with weights before being allowed in the contest line-up.

As Snyder would later put it: It wasn't that we wanted to make things difficult for the girls. We were merely determined to do away with the sort of situation that was so prevalent in New York, where you had people competing who never saw the inside of a bodybuilding gym. And we wanted to show the world what bodybuilding could do for a lady's figure."

Lori Snyder and Danny Padilla are center of attraction during a short intermission at Miss Olympia contest.

Patsy Chapman's big moment, when she was chosen over April Nicotra, second from left, and Stacey Bentley, second from right, as Best In The World. A few months later she would fail to take a place in the Miss Olympia event.

The girls were asked to perform a number of repetitions in the bench press exercise with a barbell that weighted about half of their own bodyweight. *Incredibly, very few of the girls who applied to compete in George's Best In The World contest in 1979 complained.* Indeed, the genuine bodybuilders among them welcomed the idea. Ah, but then the *Best In The World* turned out to be a kind of Pandora's Box. For it opened the door through which the previously referred to strange bodybuilding moth would fly out into the world.

Snyder recalls that the girls who competed in his *Best In The World* contest were, for the most part, beautiful advertisements for female bodybuilding. He had asked them not to strike muscle poses that reminded of their male counterparts and the greater portion of the contestants had abided by his request. But then there were one or two who decided at the last moment to do their own thing. One fairly muscular young woman from California bounded onto the stage kicked off her shoes, then proceeded to strike a number of poses that seemed to have been lifted straight out of Arnold Schwarzenegger's *Education of a Bodybuilder* textbook. There were the incredible lat spread and the double biceps and the

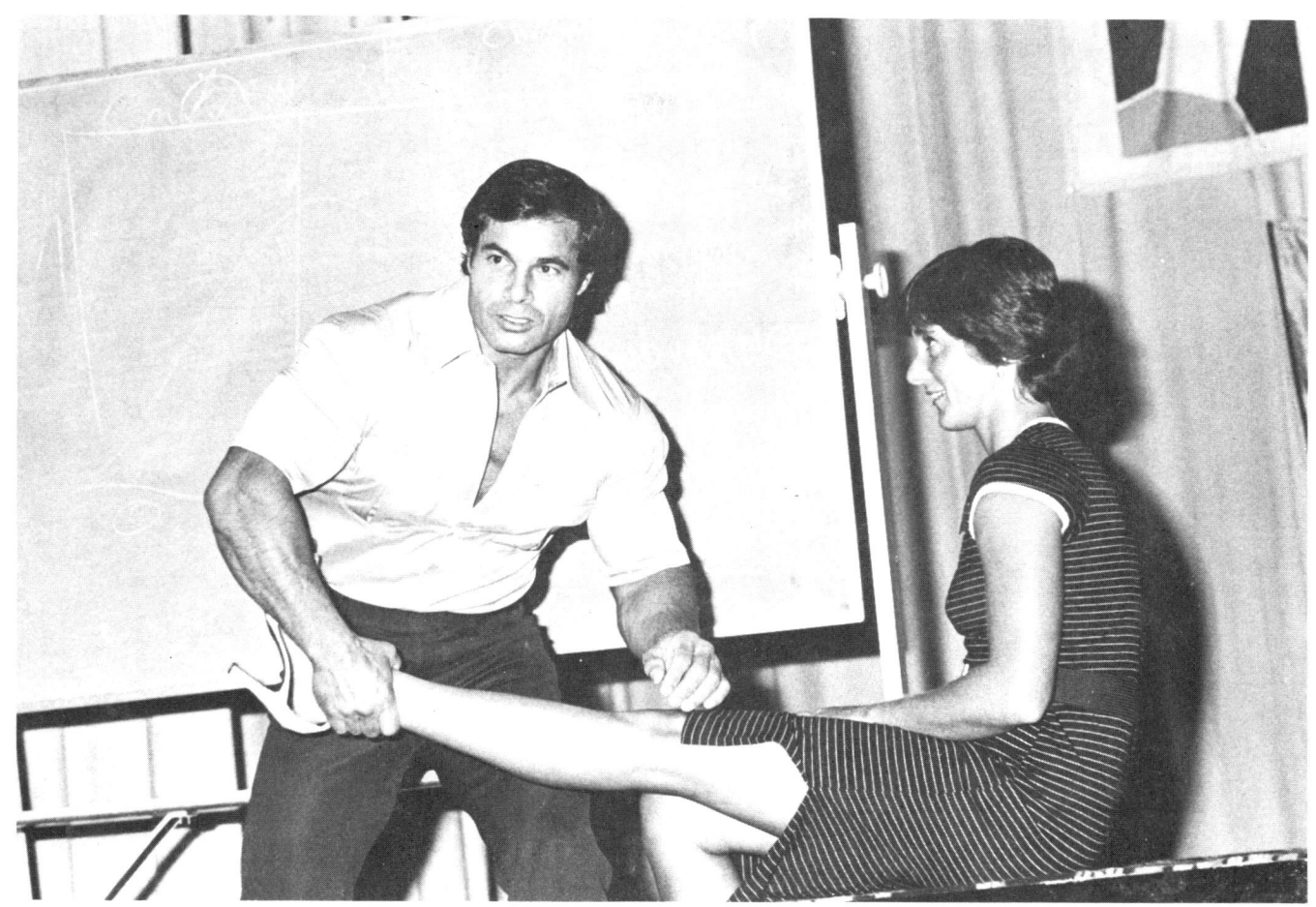

Dr. Franco Columbu explains injuries during the women's seminar held in conjunction with the Miss Olympia contest.

most muscular pose. Here was something . . . well, yes, there's only one word for it . . . freaky! And it brought the house down. The young lady had her moment onstage and she lapped up every minute of it, throwing pose after pose that showed female muscle in a fashion previously unimagined, as far as women were concerned, at any rate.

Finally the title went to gorgeous and beautifully built bodybuilder from Michigan named Patsy Chapman. Her sleek black skin, her truly incredible muscle tone and the way her doe eyes lit up her smile won the day for her. But something new had found its way into the air. Something that George Snyder and the WBA had not planned for. It took everyone by surprise. And that was only the beginning. By the time the muscle magazines got down to reporting the *Best In The World* event female bodybuilding as it had been known had taken on a new dimension. An entertaining dimension, true, but also one that left bodybuilding promoters at a complete loss what to do next. It was obvious that the patrons at Snyder's big show had enjoyed every minute of the women's contest and would eagerly snap up tickets to the next WBA promotion. But whether or not muscular women striking con-

Another view of the Miss Olympia lineup: Lorie Johnston, Patsy Chapman, Stacey Bentley and Carolyn Cheshire are closest to camera. Stacey took fifth place in contest.

ventional male postures on stage was the way to go, well that was altogether a different question that only time would decide.

Shortly after the fantastically successful *Best In The World* event Ben Weider and George Snyder decided it might well be in the best interests of bodybuilding generally to have male and female physique under the banner of the International Federation of Bodybuilders.

The IFBB is an umbrella group. While bodybuilding events around the world are conducted according to strict IFBB rules, in America amateur bodybuilding in firmly controlled by the Amateur Athletic Union (AAU), a group that not so long ago affiliated with the IFBB. Of course, professional bodybuilding in this country comes under the direct control of the IFBB.

George Snyder's discussions with the president of the IFBB soon led to more discussions with the AAU and by November of 1979 the AAU had made provisions for a women's organization that would work closely with its National Physique Association. Lisa Lyon was chosen as chairperson of the first committee to establish that organization.

The AAU vested in Lisa the responsibility to promote female bodybuilding as a competitive sport in America and Lisa vowed to do all in her power to help establish the activity according to the direction chosen by female

Patsy Chapman strikes a graceful pose for Miss Olympia judges. "You have to think about your existence away from the posing platform," she said later.

bodybuilders. Before long she was inviting other female bodybuilders to send in their ideas for establishing their sport as a serious and respected athletic activity.

It seemed female bodybuilding was off to a great start. Lisa made numerous television appearances, gave countless interviews to some of the leading American magazines and featured in newspaper articles throughout the nation. It seemed Lisa was destined to become the Arnold Schwarzenegger of bodybuilding. She was witty, affable, intelligent and bubbling with exciting femininity. Any jokes about her development would be a slap in the face of the would-be comedian. For there was nothing about Lisa that could be considered overly done. She had the lines of a well-trained dancer, but more shapely. And when she talked about the benefits of weight-training there was not an interviewer in the land who found fault in her gospel. Lisa was everything she promised. An incredible figure obvious good health and dynamic sex appeal. She appeared in *People* magazine and talked on *Merv Griffin* and *Donahue*. Where the male bodybuilder, in the early days of his sport, had to suffer the slings and arrows of every half-wit television comic before finally

Miss Olympia 1980, Rachel McLish is 24 years-old and married. She is employed by Dyna-Cam, a training equipment manufacturing company in Texas. At left, Betty Brown and Samir Bannout compare abdominals at the Olympus Gym in Warrington, Pa.

gaining media acceptance, Lisa walked triumphantly from the beginning. Soon there was hardly a bodybuilding show that appeared on television without Lisa coming on as co-host. And what a great job she performed. Wherever she appeared Lisa never left any doubt that bodybuilding with weights had served only to enhance her womanliness. True, she was firmer in the shoulders, arms and thighs than the most glamorous of the Hollywood ladies. But the tautness of her body never suggested masculinity. She was always fashionable from head to toe. And there was no reluctance on her part to wear a flower in her hair when she felt the occasion appropriate. Lipstick and nail polish were a normal part of her makeup. Yes, indeed, Lisa brought the welcome fragrance of healthy, vivacious womanhood to an otherwise sweaty atmosphere. All over America she was the bodybuilder's sweetheart, a model for countless women of all ages. She converted thousands to the bodybuilding faith and not all of them female.

Last April Lisa produced her own bodybuilding championships at the Boardwalk Regency in Atlantic City, New Jersey. The event drew some 30 contestants from all over the United States and the result was televised on NBC's Sportsworld three weeks after the fact. Rachel McLish of Texas was the winner, with Georgia Fudge of Florida second and Claudia Wilbourn of Calfornia in third place. A few days after the Lisa Lyon Women's National Championships Claudia Wilbourn was declared winner at the California championships. Her Muscular abdominals and back were a sight to behold.

A mere 16 months or so after Lisa set about establishing the sport of female bodybuilding it is common knowledge that she would be hardpressed to place sixth in a female bodybuilding contest. No, Lisa has not gone to pot, as they say. She is as attractive as ever. Indeed, when she graced the pages of a recent issue of *Playboy* magazine her form was enough to cause a mad rush to newsstands around the country. Truth is that what Lisa started has been taken to unprecedented lengths. So unprecedented that even judges of female bodybuilding contests are currently at a loss how to decide the results. Beauty has nothing whatever to do with the contests; or very little. It is a bodybuilding event, say the contestants and "we expect to be judged on the degree of muscularity and body symmetry we display on stage."

The extremely popular Stacey Bentley and Chris Dickerson reaped gold at a couples contest in Atlantic City. The event was covered by television and later featured nationally.

Bill Pearl, a leading figure in the IFBB has been quoted as saying: "The thing about women's physique contests as opposed to beauty contests is that you aren't going to be able to judge on how a woman combs her hair or what her face looks like. We're going to have to define why those women are on stage and if it's for a physique contest, and if the women are going to step up and hit poses normally associated with men bodybuilders, well, then that's her business."

Pearl admits that the hardcore women bodybuilders are not representative of any recognized and accepted standard of female beauty . . . "so when you start talking about the aesthetic value of a woman bodybuilder's body, well, you're pretty much going to have to start out from scratch."

In other words, the hardcore woman bodybuilder must set her own values and standards. Beauty has little to do with what concerns her but she is apparently undaunted by that. More and more women are turning to competitive bodybuilding, even as the judges try to figure out a way to judge them and still not come up with winners who are overly muscular and a complete turnoff to most women. After all, over and above the health aspect, bodybuilding is also big business. And it seems the hardcore women bodybuilders are bad for business.

Clearly Rachel's Dyna-Cam sponsor is as happy as the lady on winning the most important title in female bodybuilding.

Suzy Green strikes an abdominal pose during her routine and brings the house down at the Miss Olympia.

As George Snyder told *Sports Illustrated* recently: "The point of our contests is to choose the best woman bodybuilder. Our purpose has never been to pick a male impersonator." Commenting on a photograph of one leading female champion Snyder said: "I'm afraid that picture scared a lot of women away from weight-training."

Hear Bill Pearl again on the matter of judging women bodybuilding contests: "I'd get together with the other judges beforehand and make it clear whether we're judging a physique contest or a beauty contest. Are we taking overall attractiveness into account or just the development of various bodyparts. If the women want to be judged exactly as men then that's fine. But that will have to be clear. Otherwise you'll have a mess."

Christine Zane, a former Miss Americana who went on to become Miss Bikini at the London Mr. Universe contest, says: "Obviously we can't have individual promoters deciding what he or she thinks is the ideal female body. That is where the involvement of organizations like the IFBB and AAU comes in. These organizations can help by enforcing a set of standards that *everyone* agrees on." She said further that it is important that judges should be "sympathetic to the idea of women's bodybuilding."

On command, Miss Olympia contenders turn their backs on the judges.

Unfortunately, "the idea of women's bodybuilding" is constantly changing. When Christine won her titles women did not strike poses to show off muscular biceps and they were not expected to display tessellated abdominals. Such bodybuilding words as *ripped* and *cut* were reserved strictly for references to the condition of the male physique. Overall attractiveness was the name of the game.

Physique competition today means big money, thanks to the work of the IFBB, and both men and women stand to gain from serious training. For most male champions their game is synonymous with the taking of anabolic steroids. The men know only too well that there are serious side effects to taking steroids. Indeed, many are already paying the price. The powers who control female bodybuilding could be inadvertently encouraging women to take steroids when they allow extreme muscular definition, as displayed by the leading female champions these days, to be a top factor in their women's championships.

Frank and Christine Zane had their own booth that featured courses for men and women bodybuilders, books and tee shirts at Miss Olympia exhibition. Christine also acted as a judge during Miss Olympia contest.

The massiveness of female athletes from East Germany has been directly linked to their use of anabolic steroids, including testosterone, the drug used in sex-change operations. So much for the belief that women cannot develop muscles like those displayed by Mr. America contenders. After only two years there is evidence that if the current trend in female competition continues women might well be in a position to compete against male bodybuilders. Of course, these women will be different from any man has ever encountered before ... but then the women bodybuilders do appear bent on redefining the whole conventional idea of femininity anyway. And therein lies a big danger.

The Make-Up
Of A Competitor

April Nicotra had little idea what she was in for the night she turned up at Madison Square Garden to compete in the 1973 Miss Americana contest. A few days earlier she had gone to pick up tickets to that year's Mr. Olympia event, bent on meeting Arnold Schwarzenegger and Lou Ferrigno. The chaps at her gym had talked of nothing else for months: This clash of the bodybuilding giants had promised to be the most exciting since Schwarzenegger looked down the barrel of Sergio Oliva's cannon in 1971.

April remembers that having picked up her tickets from New York promoter Tom Minichello, he suggested she should enter the Miss Americana contest that would be held the same night as the Mr. Olympia. April had not heard of the Miss Americana show before Tom mentioned it and anyway she felt unqualified to participate in anything quite as big as Tom had described the contest. But Tom had said all sorts of wonderful things about April's looks and gradually she got around to thinking that perhaps competing might be fun. Besides there would be no better opportunity to meet Arnold and Lou backage.

She returned to her gym still undecided about the Miss Americana contest. But whereas she had been able to resist Minichello's sugar-talk April succumbed to the pleas of the fellows with whom she had been working out for a few months, ever since she decided to take up bodybuilding with weights at seventeen. April had moved straight into "the heavy room," determined as she was to discover how strong a girl could get, all of that for a school paper. Before long she was working part-time at the gym, growing stronger than she ever imagined possible, loving the whole thing but never once considering beauty contests.

April Nicotra

Well, now her gym buddies were pleading with her to enter the Miss Americana event, and April did not have the strength to let them down. She turned up at Madison Square Garden on the remembered Saturday evening uncertain what to expect. Minichello had told her only that the Miss Americana was different from the usual Miss America pageant, that contenders appeared once only before the judges, that they wore swimsuits, not dresses or evening gowns. The whole emphasis was on body development, Tom told April, and each contender was expected to show her physique to best advantage.

Years later April would recall that there were about twelve other girls in the 1973 Miss Americana and that only three or four of those had ever done any bodybuilding. The rest had been talked into competing for one non-bodybuilding reason or another. Some seemed bent on teasing the mainly male audience out of their sanity, and others appeared shy and lost. April Nicotra had no difficulty whatever winning the title of Miss Americana 1973.

It had been a fun experience. Indeed, she had enjoyed herself to such an extent the fellows at her gym had little trouble persuading her to compete again in 1974. The publicity she had received from her adventure in 1973 had been very good indeed for her gym and, doubtless, April must have seen the Miss Americana as a stepping stone to bigger things.

There are many who would like a return to the kind of figure displayed here by April Nicotra. With new criteria now being set up by the IFBB only time will tell the future of the new sport. Above, April wins the 1978 Miss United States title.

An instructor at Warrington's Olympus Gym, April goes through a routine with French bodybuilding and movie star Serge Nubret. More of April at left.

Moreover, the contest was further incentive to train regularly. Even though the caliber of contestant improved in 1974 April Nicotra again walked away with the title and landed on the pages of a number of bodybuilding magazines. In just two years she would become as well known among bodybuilders as Arnold Schwarzenegger, himself!

April might well have continued her winning streak had she not decided to participate only as a judge in the next couple of Miss Americana events. Meanwhile she was reaping the benefits of bodybuilding with weights. She recalls that although she handled really heavy poundages during workouts, contrary to what friends had predicted, she never developed huge muscle mass. She grew much stronger, true, especially in the legs, and that helped as far as her competitive skiing and running were concerned. Her calves rounded out from all the specialized work and her thighs became firmer and shaplier. Her waist retained its smallness and the exercises that she performed for her pectoral muscles resulted in a firmer bustline. Little wonder that April found herself the centre of attraction not only at bodybuilding promotions but at the beach as well.

Then George Snyder invited her to compete in his Miss Eastern United States. George had been particularly careful about the entries to this contest and so April found herself up against a fairly high caliber of competition. No matter, she got the nod from the judges and ended up on top. She would compete on two other occasions, once in a Miss United States staged by Snyder, with the same result. She always came out number one.

And then came Snyder's Best in the World event, an affair that carried money prizes of some $20,000 and a lot of valuable publicity. The contest drew contenders from all over the United States, even though Snyder's conditions were quite demanding. He had asked would-be contenders to send in black and white photographs of themselves in swimsuit so as to be properly appraised. All aspirants had to prove they were regular weight-trainers.

The contest was held in conjunction with another for male bodybuilders and this combo guaranteed a packed house. Every bodybuilding celebrity in the United States seemed to be present at the Pennsylvania show. Joe Weider and his brother Ben were there, as were Frank and Christine Zane. The judges were among the most knowledgeable in bodybuilding and Snyder left it to them to decide on the criteria for winning. However, he had previously asked the female contenders not to emulate the males. That is, he did not want them striking those postures normally associated with male physique competition.

Snyder would say later that he was amazed at the reaction to the female bodybuilders. "In the first place," he said, "I had never seen females display such a degree of muscular development. Save for one or two, most of the girls were on the slender side, But the degree of muscular definition they displayed was almost intimidating. Some had developed their midsections to a degree that surpassed that of some of the better known male champions."

But the biggest surprise, for Snyder, was the audience reaction to the more muscular girls. As they came on the fans whistled and cheered, often entreating them to hit poses that previously were seen only at events for male bodybuilders.

The whole thing rose to fever pitch when one young woman with a particularly heavy build stepped onto the platform. Encouraged by the audience, she kicked off her shoes then swung into a number of numbing postures that no other girl had dared before, not publicly. Except for her bikini top there was little about this young woman to set her apart from her male counterpart.

If Mike Wuko and Mike McVan had their way, April Nicotra would have won the Best In The World title. They had to be satisfied with second place and a chance to pose with their favorite after the contest.

"I could not believe my eyes," George Snyder would say afterwards. "And I was even more surprised by the ovation she received from the audience."

But that young woman, who was clearly the hit of the show, did not win. Instead, the money and the title went to Patsy Chapman of Michigan.

"That does not mean Patsy wasn't muscular," says April Nicotra in recalling the contest. "Her body was very firm and there was a minimum of fat over her muscles. When she stood relaxed, however, all you saw was a beautifully shaped woman with all the curves normally associated with the female. Only when she flexed her thighs or her arms did you see her weight-trained muscles. And Patsy was not huge. Certainly she did not show 15-inch biceps and abdominals that were ripped."

April placed second in the Best in the World. For some time after that she actually considered giving up bodybuilding contests, for already it was obvious a new trend had been established in female bodybuilding: The magazines were beginning to feature muscular women in a way that was never enjoyed by the Miss Americana winners and April found herself wondering whether or not it was worth changing all her ideas merely to fly with the strange new moths.

She knew from experience and study that women could not naturally develop the kind of muscularity that had been displayed at the Best in the World contest. She had learned from backstage gossip and from talking with some of the contenders that a number of girls were taking anabolic steroids in pursuit of the sort of muscularity that won contests. But April also knew there were disastrous side effects concommitant with taking such hormone drugs. She decided to have yet another try at competition, convinced that the winning standard of Patsy Chapman was within her reach. She set her sights on the Miss Olympia 1980 event that George Snyder would stage at the Sheraton in Philadelphia.

"I trained harder for this one than I had ever done before," April recalls. "I ran and I worked out at the gym six days a week. I was particularly careful with my diet and I handled more weights than ever before. But I simply could not develop the muscle striations or the kind of muscular definition that I saw displayed by the various winners featured in the muscle magazines."

She was more than ever convinced that some of the girls really were taking dangerous hormone treatments in their pursuit of muscularity that reminded of the male champions of bodybuilding. But April remained undaunted. By September of 1980, days before the Miss Olympia contest, she had hit what she considered winning condition. She was in the best shape of her eight-year bodybuilding career and brimming with confidence. If Patsy Chapman was the standard required by the judges, she thought, then she would be ready for the best of them come Miss Olympia day.

April Nicotra, twice Miss Americana, twice Miss Eastern United States, and Miss United States came to Philadelphia prepared for victory. She had spent hours each day perfecting her posing routine, her skin was in impeccable condition and her body appeared almost fat-free. Her thighs, always her best physical feature, had never looked better. She had developed a superb tan that was highlighted by a beautifully-cut bikini, discovered after weeks of searching the best boutiques in New York.

So now she was finally ready to face the girl from Michigan who a few months earlier had been adjudged *Best in the World*, Patsy Chapman. All she had to do was surpass Patsy and the bodybuilding world would be her oyster.

George Butler, co-author of the bestseller **Pumping Iron,** *takes a shot of Patsy Chapman from his own vantage point. Patsy is dynamite from any angle, say her fans.*

How was April to know that by the time she took her place in the Miss Olympia lineup female bodybuilding would have taken still another direction, a direction never before imagined even by the promoters of such events

Lorie Johnston sat in row three, a few feet from, Snyder's *Best in the World* stage, quietly taking in what had set near to three thousand other people on the edge of their seats. She watched in silence as Laura Coombes of Florida went through her posing routine, wondered how a girl could develop such muscular mass and definition, wondered *why* so many were applauding her efforts.

She saw Patsy Chapman walk gracefully to the posing platform, eyes ablaze with the excitement of the evening, self-confidence radiating around her. Lorie remembers thinking how like a sleek panther Patsy moved from one pose to the next and how she never once let you forget that she was all woman. Lorie wondered whether, like herself, Patsy was a student of dance. She moved with such rhythm.

Lorie Johnston, a dancer who trains with weights, was confident she would do well in the 1980 Miss Olympia. But even in the flawless condition pictured here she failed to place. She appeared on national television later to demonstrate the training routine that she had used in her Miss Olympia preparations.

Lorie Johnston

Lorie was particularly interested in April Nicotra's performance. The two had trained together at Snyder's Olympus Gym for three months or so, April in preparation for this *Best in the World* contest, Lorie as a means of strengthening those muscles that took such a beating from dancing.

Indeed, from watching April at the gym Lorie had begun to think it might be fun to compete in the contests that had made April such a popular figure in bodybuilding. She had competed with some success in one or two beauty pageants at local beach resorts but at 18 she did not have April's experience. By watching April, by training with her, Lorie hoped to follow in her footsteps. If that did not work out, she thought, then the gym work would certainly pay off where her dancing was concerned.

So as April now mounted the posing platform Lorie felt a lump rise in her throat. It was as if she were herself about to step up before this excited crowd to be judged; to be applauded or largely ignored.

April's performance reflected the hours of preparation that great posing routines always demand. And for once Lorie Johnston found herself applauding ecstatically. A win for April on this night would practically amount to a personal victory for Lorie. It was at the end of April's presentation that Lorie Johnston decided once and for all that she would compete in the next event George Snyder staged in her area.

And so, three days after the *Best in the World* title went to Michigan's Patsy Chapman, Lorie Johnston began her own preparations for an assault on the biggest, most important title in all of female bodybuilding.

She had been blessed by nature with a bone structure that was neither too large nor too slender. She had a healthy complexion that was free of blemish, never mind that she had just turned eighteen. And dancing had formed her legs firm, from hip to ankle.

She was careful about her training program. Where April Nicotra performed set after set of situps for her abdominals, Lorie practiced twists to further whittle down her naturally slim waist. She had discovered that when she performed situps her waist measurement increased. She did very little bench pressing, for she already had a full bust. Instead she performed sets of cable crossovers, bent arm laterals on a flat bench, dumbbells in her hands.

She had learned from training with April Nicotra that bodybuilding routines had to be designed to a girl's specific needs.

By mid-August Lorie felt confident enough to allow herself to believe she might well be able to pull off what her friend and training partner had failed to achieve at the *Best in the World* contest. She would say after the Miss Olympia that she entered believing she was at least as good as the best in the *Best in the World*. Lorie Johnston had a surprise coming.

At the Best In The World event there were clear signs of things to come. Note Stacey Bentley's and Carla Dunlap's abdominal muscularity.

A backstage picture that tells a million words about successful bodybuilding. Frank Zane, three times winner of the Mr. Olympia title, poses with Rachel McLish.

The Miss Olympia Contest

"Bodybuilding for men has come a very long way," said Arnold at the Miss Olympia contest, *"and now we must do all in our power to properly establish the sport for the female participants."* Wild applause greeted the pledge.

For George Snyder the Miss Olympia contest in 1980 promised to be the peak of a five-year career as a bodybuilding promoter. He had begun with his Mr. and Miss Eastern United States, back in 1976. With Arnold Schwarzenegger as his guest star, at a time when Arnold was appearing regularly on television, when *Pumping Iron* was still the talk of the movie crowd, he felt certain of success. Of course, he had not bargained on the quantity of hard work involved but finally he had taken the whole thing in his stride. Certainly, in the end the whole thing had seemed well worth the effort. Indeed, things had gone well enough to encourage Snyder to try his hand at promoting a second and third time.

Stacey Bentley and Georgia Miller Fudge display on "AM-Philadelphia" what Miss Olympia patrons would later see in the flesh.

By the time he had staged his Mr. and Miss United States, however, Snyder had begun to look at female bodybuilding with more interested eyes than he had turned on regular male physique competition. That area, as he saw it, had already been well and truly cornered. There was not all that much new that he could bring to the sport. The International Federation of Bodybuilders, under its untiring president, Ben Weider, had done an incredible organizational job in the last five years or so, professional bodybuilding had gradually risen from the ground floor of sport to the penthouse, with the stars making more money in a year than they ever imagined possible. The Mr. Olympia had found its way into televisionland and the pages of America's leading journals. *Rolling Stone* had actually sent a team to South Africa to film the contest.

But female bodybuilding was still a little caterpillar in a cocoon that refused to open up. As George came to see it finally, there was little he could do to make a mark on bodybuilding, male bodybuilding that is. Everything had already been done that could be done, he thought. But female bodybuilding, well, here was something that could do with a little bit of help.

Cathy Gelfo and Christine Zane confer with IFBB president Ben Weider regarding judging procedures for the Miss Olympia contest in 1980.

Of course, he had set up his Women's Bodybuilding Association with some success. But then Ben Weider had talked him into bringing his efforts under the IFBB banner, a good move. With Ben's cooperation Snyder had been able to spread his bodybuilding gospels throughout the world via the IFBB's own journal, *Muscle Builder*, now renamed *Muscle & Fitness*.

Joining the IFBB had also brought Snyder closer to the leading people in male and female bodybuilding, helped establish Snyder as a major promoter.

So Snyder looked at the bodybuilding scene and then he decided to put all of his promotional abilities into that area which, as far as he was concerned, appeared most in need of a shot in the arm. Women bodybuilding. He thought again and came up with the idea of the Miss Olympia contest, which would be the biggest thing for the ladies, in much the same way that the Mr. Olympia had become bodybuilding's Super Bowl.

The idea appealed to Ben Weider immediately and he encouraged Snyder in his efforts, giving whatever help he could from time to time.

The big winners in the Miss Olympia 1980 title. Said Rachel McLish afterwards, "You'd be surprised at the amount of complimentary whistles I get when I walk down the street." — No we wouldn't!

As Snyder would say later, even as the *Best In The World* contest was coming to a close he was already planning his publicity campaign for the 1980 Miss Olympia. He had had talks with theater owners in New York and Philadelphia, had faced the prospect of spending a small fortune keeping up with union demands and so on. And finally he had decided it would be in the best interests of all concerned with the Miss Olympia if he staged the event at the Sheraton Hotel in Philadelphia.

Certainly the hotel offered a different setting from the usual bodybuilding venue. It would mean bringing in his own sound system and lighting, yes, but no other place he had visited boasted as excellent a catering service. Besides, the people that George Snyder spoke with at the Philadelphia Sheraton had been so very cooperative in every way. George booked the hotel days after the successful conclusion of his *Best In The World* contest

Next he sent out his invitations to the leading stars of female bodybuilding: Georgia Miller Fudge of St. Petersburg, Florida, Stacey Bentley of Santa Monica, California, Rachel McLish of Texas, Patsy Chapman, Cammie Lusko, Lynn Conkwright among them.

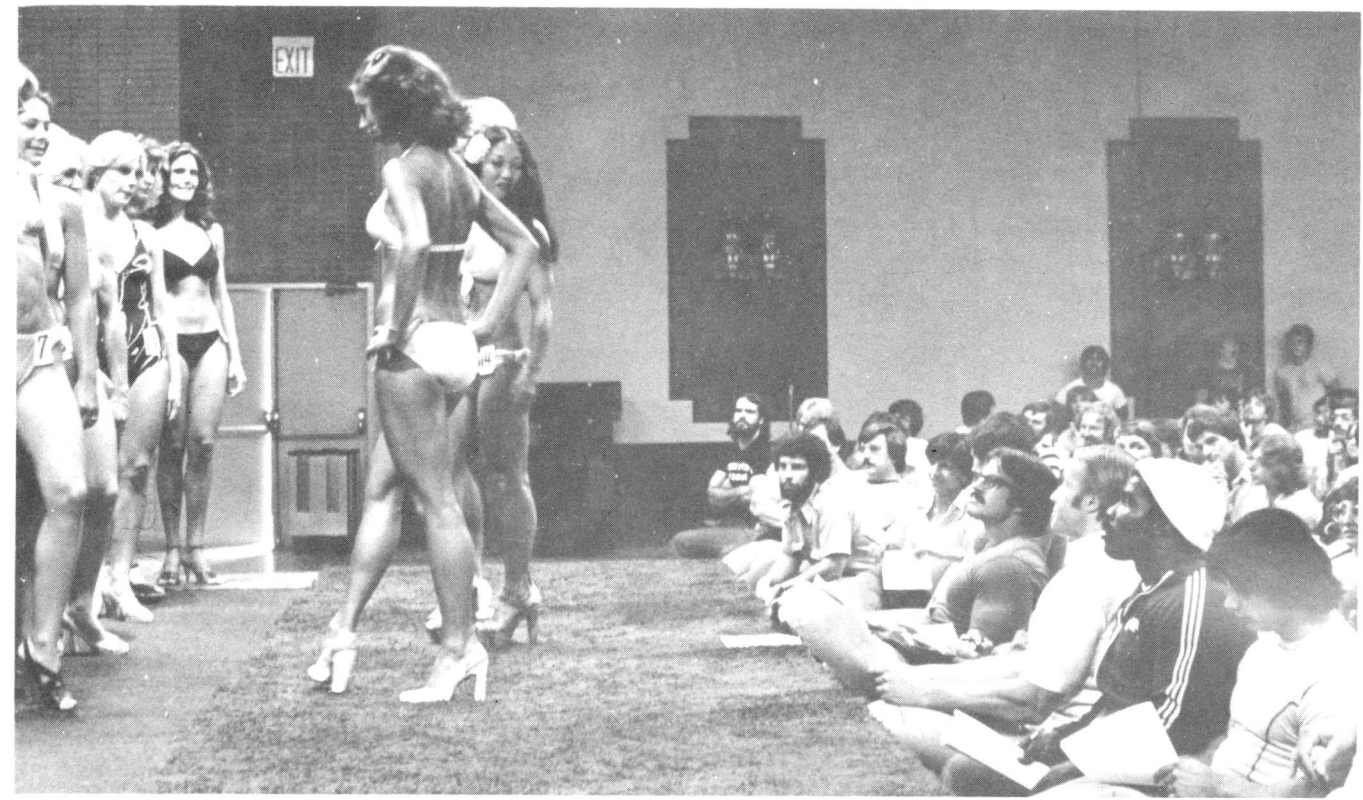

To judge the ladies of bodybuilding, Snyder invited some of the most knowledgeable in the field, including Mike Katz, a former Mr. America; Doris Barrilleaux; Damon Poole, Mr. Universe; Christine Zane (who had by then relinquished her position on the IFBB's female bodybuilding committee); Dr. Dan Howard; Sevn-Ole Thorsen of Denmark, gym owner and publisher of a bodybuilding magazine; and Valerie Coe, wife of Boyer Coe, a Mr. Universe winner.

Snyder also invited Cathy Gelfo, the secretary of the IFBB's female bodybuilding committee.

On the day of the contest Christine Zane produced a number of guidelines for judging the bodybuilders. These were turned down by the judging panel. Instead, a number of suggestions by Lisa Lyon (who already was becoming a rare commodity), published in *Muscle Fitness* and apparently endorsed by the IFBB, were adopted. Girls would come out as called and on command would do four turns (front, side, back, side), as a group.

Round two would consist of fixed poses, done individually. Each pose would allow the contender to show her physique to best advantage. Suggested sequence: front chest pose, front arm pose, front leg pose, left side twisting pose, back pose with arms overhead, back pose with arms down, back leg pose with emphasis on calves, right side twisting pose.

Miss USA was one of the first contests for female bodybuilders that George Snyder promoted. Note that contenders were then allowed to wear shoes.

Rick Wayne and Arnold Schwarzenegger at Miss Olympia prejudging.

The final round would consist of a lineup, followed by a single freestyle posing routine, approximately one minute in duration. The routine would consist of poses each of which emphasized a particular muscle group.

It was pointed out that "it should be remembered that this is a bodybuilding competition and over-reliance on elements outside the sport, that is, dance, gymnastics etc, should not be favored. Attire should consist of a minimal two-piece bathing suit, no shoes, a minimum of jewelry, no other ornamentation, tasteful makeup, with the hair preferably up or back if the hair is long."

In time Snyder himself would say he had no part in the setting up of the criteria by which the Miss Olympia contenders would be judged. That was left to Cathy Gelfo and the IFBB, under whose colors the contest was being organized.

However, Snyder's very personal view was that it seemed to him all the factors that made a woman different from a man had been clipped out.

"I saw nothing wrong in a woman picking a hairstyle that suited her and there was no reason to expect women not to wear high heels with their bikini," he said. "But it was a matter for the judges and the officers of the IFBB. My personal feelings in no way influenced the choosing of Miss Olympia."

The judging of the contest was a long drawn-out affair. It took four hours, during which time the girls hit poses that were similar in many ways to those normally seen at male muscle contests. And clearly the rule about gymnastic performances was not adhered to.

At this point I should say that I had been living in the Caribbean for most of 1979 and part of 1980 when female bodybuilding took off in America. I kept in touch with bodybuilding generally through the magazines and regular telephone conversations with George Snyder, however. I returned to the states especially to witness the Miss Olympia contest for the purposes of this book and walked straight into Mars. At least, I felt I had walked into a completely alien environment when I stepped into the lobby of the Philadelphia Sheraton.

All around me there were people in sweat suit bottoms and tank tops that suggested the wearers were not male and yet somehow they were not by their physical appearance female either. They were for the most part extremely muscular, all tanned deep brown and obviously very excited.

In time I would bump into Patsy Chapman, who I recognized from her many published photographs, April Nicotra and Stacey Bentley, who had transformed her body in the short time I had been away from the bodybuilding scene, and in the process acquired star status in the sport. When I told her I hardly recognized her, Stacey said thanks a lot and meant it. It would not have done to say otherwise. For by her own description she was fat and out of shape two years earlier.

I sat through the pre-judging of the Miss Olympia, all the while fighting everything within me that suggested what I was looking at was a scene from some weird science fiction movie. I tried to relive the old days when male bodybuilders were looked upon by the masses as a bunch of over-developed freaks, which clearly we thought we were not. And I told myself that perhaps I was allowing conventional prejudices to get the better of me.

At one point I hypnotized myself into operating with a clear mind. I would try to look at this new female bodybuilding thing with *open* eyes, I promised myself. This was a new sport, nothing like anything I had ever experienced, said the new little voice in my head. There were new rules, new criteria. It should not be judged by anything that went before. Yeah?

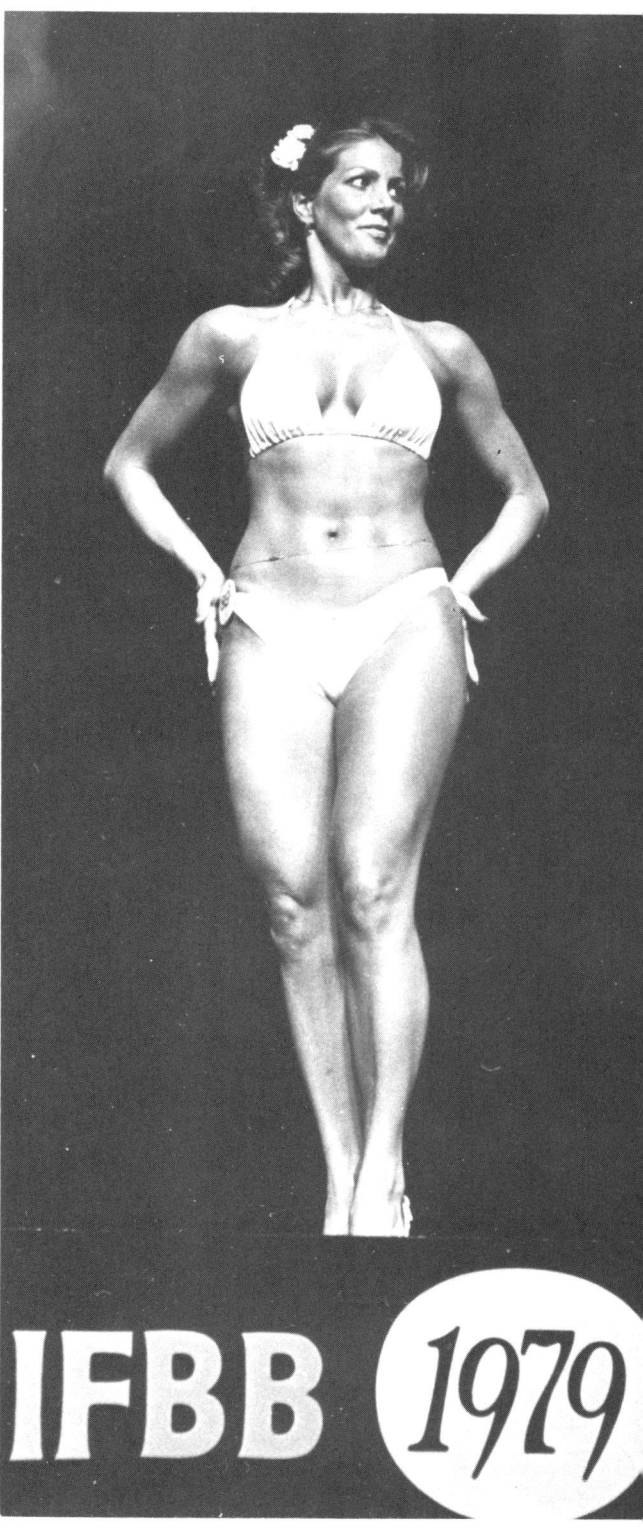

The delectable Miss April Nicotra, winner of two Miss Americana contests, Miss Eastern United States and Miss USA.

Auby Paulick (third from left) treats Miss Olympia judges to an amazing view; clearcut abdominals seldom displayed even by male physique champions.

Hard as I tried I could not forget that the people who threw most muscular poses before me, poses that were everything like those I had myself hit in competition, were female. Women, for crying out loud. People to make love to, to caress and yes, feel up. I tried to imagine making love to one of these people with biceps that were as muscular as any Mr. Universe's I had ever witnessed. I gazed in absolute wonder at the abdominal muscularity so many of the ladies displayed before the judging panel. And still I could not accept as normal, whatever that word means, what I saw. No excuse I offered seemed to make sense. Women simply were never meant to look like that!

Then Patsy Chapman came up to pose before the judges. Ah, I thought, so they were not all like *that*. And I felt relieved. She posed with grace and in her own way reminded of a gazelle, those wide open eyes of hers, her high cheek bones and bubbling personality, making me feel as a normal male likely feels at the sight of an attractive, healthy female.

She turned around so the judges could better view her back and calves and my own eyes greedily devoured her firm round buttocks, the curve of her hips, the tight skin back of her thighs. Patsy has shoulders that are perhaps

April Nicotra and Serge Nubret during the interview portion of the prime time TV show that was filmed at the Olympus Gym.

wider than the average girl's. But those are bones, friend, not thick muscular deltoids. So her shoulders do not remind of a football player or boxer. Nothing about her presentation threatened the male in me. Neither did her body offend my senses.

I thought April Nicotra, when her turn came to pose, looked more muscular that I remembered her. But there were no deep striations across her breasts. And while her thighs were harder looking than before they were nonetheless still attractive. But the postures that she adopted for the judges gave me reason for pause. I could not understand why she was apparently trying to look like Arnold Schwarzenegger, could not understand why she had to do poses to show off her biceps muscles. After all, the conventional beauty goddess is not famous because she has particularly muscular biceps.

One young woman impressed me quite a bit. She was the closest thing to the conventional idea of a beautifully built woman. I remember suggesting to the person who sat next to me at the pre-judging of the Miss Olympia that

Undaunted by her failure to place in the 1980 Miss Olympia contest, Lorie Johnston continues to train regularly, determined at 18 to rise to the top of her chosen sport.

this girl would have been highly appreciated at the London Miss Universe. Her waist was tiny, firm and it curved naturally into her hips. There was clearly a layer of fat over her body but that did not in any way take away from her sensuous beauty . . . Somehow it made her seem normal. Yes, I guess I was still somehow associating sex with female body beauty. If that makes me abnormal, I nevertheless admit my guilt.

I would discover later that the young woman previously referred to was named Lorie Johnston, the one who trained with April Nicotra but who had a completely different sort of figure.

For reasons that I would discover much later nearly all of the women at the Miss Olympia pre-judging were flat-chested and without the shapely behind normally associated with females. It made a welcome change to set eyes on Lorie Johnston.

Some of the Miss Olympia contenders had chests that lived close to grotesque. Their bikini tops, in many cases served only to draw attention to their lack of anything vaguely resembling a woman's bustline. And those who showed something in their bra cups . . . well, what they showed looked suspiciously foreign. As if, in desperation they had taken themselves to surgeon and paid him to refill their bosoms with silicone. When these ladies flexed their chest muscles the audience saw a weird scene, with muscular pectorals that split under pressure up to a point, then suddenly rose up again where the foreign element had been introduced.

I left the pre-judging not totally convinced the fault wasn't with me. Perhaps I still had to cleanse my mind of conventional male-female attitudes. But then I would ask myself later, why shouldn't I follow my male instincts. After all, there was no one mold from which women were made. Nature had taken care of every male fancy, in the same way that every female fancy had been catered to. That was why some guys went for fat women and others for skinny woman and still others for women of athletic builds. But this was altogether something new. Perhaps in the end bodybuilding would force us males to redefine womanhood and femininity. What a day!

Danny Padilla and Mike Mentzer are two physique stars who strongly support female bodybuilding. Both conducted seminars at the Philadelphia Sheraton in advance of the Miss Olympia event.

Joe and Ben Weider proudly display plaques awarded them at Miss Olympia, ". . . in recognition of their untiring efforts for bodybuilding worldwide." At left is Allan Dalfen, president of Weider Barbell Co., center is Lloyd Lambert Jr., and at right, Lloyd Lambert Sr., owners of Dyna-Cam plus sponsors of the 1980 Miss Olympia contest. And obviously, that's Rachel sharing her happiest moment with these VIP's.

The Sheraton ballroom had been set up as a high class restaurant at show time. George Snyder had deliberately steered away from the conventional theater atmosphere for his bodybuilding show. And it seemed not one of the three thousand or so faces I saw at the dining tables was without a happy smile. I took my place at a table with Leroy Colbert, the former Mr. America, Joe and Ben Weider, Joe's wife. Dennis Tinerino a Mr. Universe winner sat nearby.

Following a sumptuous repast that included the most delicious chicken this writer has ever tasted, I settled down to watch the Miss Olympia show. I say show because the contest had already been judged earlier in the day and the judges had more or less decided the order of the winners.

The affair began with MC Len Bosland announcing that "for those who may be wondering how the contest was judged, let me say it was judged in the same way that male bodybuilding contests are decided. Judges look for muscular definition, good posing and body symmetry." Bosland, as it turned out later, was correct only to a point. But we will come to that later.

As is the custom, as each lady took over the spotlight the MC revealed pertinent details of her bodybuilding background. Stacey Bentley was 23 years old, formerly

Stacey Bentley in action.

from Pennsylvania. She moved to Santa Monica, California, two years earlier to be in the swim of bodybuilding things. And she had quickly achieved success. Having won two top championships, she had received extensive media coverage, with TV appearances on the *Merv Griffin Show* and *Eyewitness Los Angeles* to her credit. She had been featured in *Time* magazine, *Playgirl* and the *London Star*. Like other contenders who would follow he onstage, Stacey wore a very brief bikini, no jewelry and her hair had been neatly cut. She was shoeless.

Few male bodybuilding champions ever receive the applause that greeted Stacey's appearance on stage. Thanks to *Muscle & Fitness*, by now the bodybuilder's bible, she was a superstar of her sport.

Then there was Patsy Chapman, who had won acclaim at Snyder's *Best In The World* contest a few months earlier. Relaxed she appeared taut but save for her abdominals, which were barely discernible under her near fat-free skin, little muscle showed. When Patsy flexed her legs or her back, however, the story was altogether different. Now you knew she was no ordinary gymnast or dancer. It was clear then that she had put her body through the rigors of regular workouts with heavy barbells and dumbbells.

Patsy Chapman

It seemed Patsy Chapman had decided not to strike the usual male oriented postures on stage. Well, say it straight, she hit a few but there was always that little twist that made them, well, *different.* You did not mind what she did because, somehow, Patsy added a feminine quality to her poses. Her side chest pose, for example, did not remind of Robby Robinson. Rather, you saw an obviously healthy and strong female displaying female lines, it with a marked difference from the usual picture.

According to Len Bosland, Patsy came from Port Huron, Michigan. She was 21 years old at five feet, five inches. Her bodyweight was given as 128 pounds. At the time of her appearance she had been studying journalism and telecommunications at Michigan State University.

Carolyn Cheshire had come all the way from Britain for a crack at the Miss Olympia money. A former *Vogue* model, she now ran an exercise class six days her week in her native country. Her form had added special spice to the title sequences of the last four James Bond movies.

Carolyn was one of the few contenders for the Miss Olympia title who did not sport a tan. The English weather being what it is she had not had the opportunity to go brown in time for the contest. She presented an extremely lean figure but there was none of the muscularity displayed earlier by Stacey Bentley. Indeed, hers was the figure of a dancer even though the poses she offered come right out of *Muscle & Fitness* magazine.

Georgia Miller Fudge was a very popular contender and the reason was clear. Tall and beautifully tanned, she also had the long shapely legs and flowing blonde hair that added up to the Beach Boys vision of the California girl. But Georgia is a native of St. Petersburg, Florida. At 34 years of age she had mothered two teenagers. She owned and operated a very successful gym with her husband Dick, who had trained a number of leading male champions, Jim Haislop among them.

Already Georgia was Miss Olympus, Miss Body Beautiful and Miss Temple Terrace. You could not say Georgia Fudge looked anything like a man. No sir, for she had rounded breasts that showed enough of themselves beneath her strategically cut bikini top. She had a small waist that was tightly muscled and her hips curved in the manner of conventional womanhood. Ah, but when Georgia posed her muscles jumped up at you aggressively, rudely interrupting any libidinous fantasy journeys that, at the sight of her, your stupid imagination

*Carolyn Cheshire and
Georgia Miller Fudge*

may have set out on. Like the other girls, Georgia posed to her own music and the uninhibited whistles and cheers of the audience.

When Auby Paulick bounced onto the stage you were not certain how to react. Somehow she reminded of Joan Rivers, the comedienne. She had this infectious smile that drew her audience easily into her corner. Her personality bubbled like finest quality champagne. It was hard to imagine a boring evening in her company. She sang with the music that she had chosen for her posing routine. Yes, Auby seemed as exciting a female (pardon my natural . . . or are they *un*-natural drives!) as any man could conjure in his mind.

Auby displayed incredible abdominal development . . .

Auby Paulick

She moved with all the grace of a ballet star. Yes, and when she flexed her incredibly muscular abdominal muscles it was with the ease of a lioness lapping up water from some movie oasis. Somehow you gradually forgot the woman in Auby as she cavorted around the platform. She performed near impossible feats of agility, splits, handstands . . . And she flexed her back and her intercostals and her calves so that the muscles seemed to jump from the stage at your throat.

I turned around for a look at Joe Weider's face. After all, his magazine had publicized this new sport as no other had. He saw me studying him and Joe smiled, as if to let me know that he knew exactly what I was thinking. The look on his beauty queen wife's face was more to the point. A former popular covergirl, Betty Weider was clearly at a loss what to make of the spectacle under the posing light.

The audience would not let Auby leave at the end of her presentation. They carried on to such an extent that the muscular lady was forced to return for a repeat performance.

Cammie Lusko

All day long the writer had heard from observers at the pre-judging that Cammie Lusko was facially, the most attractive contender for the Miss Olympia title. They also said she had the body of a young male. She held her shoulders square, that was true, and even as she stood relaxed in the lineup with the other competitors there was something about her that was, well, unusual. She appeared very powerful. Word was that she could easily press with one hand a dumbbell that weighed 110 pounds! Perhaps Cammie's walk had a lot to do with the way so many described her. Not for her the hip swaying manner of so many contest hopefuls. She walked straight, arms held away from her body (which accounted for the square shoulders look), every tanned pore exuding power . . . power not normally associated with a woman.

Len Bosland told his audience Cammie was 22 years old, that she was a stuntgirl who appeared in *Buck Rodgers*, besides being a tennis instructor. She had also competed in a number of bodybuilding contests across the USA.

Rachel McLish

Cammie offered a number of splits, big biceps poses and lat spreads. She also flashed a beautiful smile now and then that, added to her very attractive face and curls, served to further confuse those who preferred not to see the woman in her.

And then Rachel McLish came on. The proud possessor of a B.S. degree in Physical and Health Education, not to mention the holder of the U.S. Women's Bodybuilding Champion 1980 title, she arrived under the spotlight beaming with self-confidence. Next to Auby Paulick, Rachel presented the most muscular body of the evening . . . and it was clear, judging by audience reaction to her every move, that the two mentioned would battle for first place in the end. Rachel offered few gymnastic moves and there were no handstands or pirouettes. But the poses she struck proved conclusively that women can build muscular bodies that only a few men might equal.

Rachel McLish — Miss Olympia
Frank Zane — Mr. Olympia

It was clearly not Lorie Johnston's night. Nor April Nicotra's. For obviously what the audience had come out to see was muscle comparable to what they were used to enjoying at male contests. It seemed the fans had come out to view a bodybuilding contest not to be confused with a beauty pageant. By their uninhibited reaction it was clear the fans were not all that concerned with pretty faces or graceful poses. The more hard muscle you shoved in their faces they better they appreciated it.

At one point, former Mr. America Leroy Colbert leaned over and whispered in my ear: "What the hell *is* this?" he asked, obviously perplexed. The popular voice was so obviously behind those girls who had displayed the muscles with the deepest ridges and cuts. You got the feeling that had Arnold Schwarzenegger donned a bikini and mounted the posing platform few of those in the audience would have noticed the difference. They came out to see muscle and it seemed to matter not one damn whether the exhibit wore a bikini or a pair of briefs.

It came as no surprise when Len Bosland announced the victory of Rachel McLish. For some reason she had pipped Auby Paulick, a desicision that did not please all of the audience. Third and fourth places went to Lynn Conkwright and Corrine Machado.For once Stacey Bentley had to be satisfied with fifth position.

Sandy Connors is a successful model and real estate agent. She finds time to indulge her love for ballet and jazz even though she trains five times a week and competes in events like the Miss Olympia.

Obviously the flesh was more than willing but George Snyder's eyes were beginning to call it a day after a hard day's night of Miss Olympia feasting. Photographer Craig Deitz was wide awake, however.

The losers stood behind the winners for a few minutes while the photographers clicked away, then they left the stage to Frank Zane, three times Mr. Olympia, and Rachel McLish. The two then posed together, to indescribable joy of the audience. Candidly, there were times when I thought Rachel clearly outmuscled Frank . . . but that might not necessarily have been the lady's fault.

Yes, finally Patsy Chapman, who had been declared the best woman bodybuilder in the world some months earlier, had failed even to take a place among the first five winners at the Miss Olympia. Bodybuilding had taken a new direction for women. Muscle, clearly defined, ripped to shreds muscle, was now the name of the game. And that which had set Patsy apart from the other girls earlier was now not nearly good enough to take a place in the new race. April Nicotra and Lorie Johnston would now have to decide whether or not they wished to follow the leaders in this totally new ballgame. I would talk to them, to Patsy Chapman, to the losers and the winners, later.

A short while before the Miss Olympia, Georgia Fudge was second to Rachel McLish. On Olympia day, however, it was a totally different picture.

How They Took It

Georgia Fudge didn't mind losing to Rachel McLish. It was not the first time that the 24-year-old Texas champion had made it past Georgia to the number one spot. Indeed, a few months earlier Georgia had placed second to Rachel and felt pretty good about it. After all, she was mother to a 16-year-old daughter and a 14-year-old son back in St. Petersburg, Florida. But not to have placed at all in the Miss Olympia that Rachel had won was a lot to take. And Georgia was not certain how to explain the result.

"Yesterday somebody said I ought not to be competing against these young people," she revealed, in a controlled fit of depression. "Perhaps I should heed that advice. I don't know . . . I have done well in the past."

Her husband was more to the point. A gym owner and sometime trainer of champions, he blamed Georgia's misfortune in failing to place in the Miss Olympia on the judges. Well, not quite. They had not really seen his wife he said.

Until the new emphasis on clearcut muscularity, Montreal's Mimi Rivest was riding high as a leading contender for top honors. She failed to place in Philadelphia but promises to be back.

"You get an invitation to compete in a big contest," he explained, "you are told there won't be a whole lot of nobodies. You train like hell, you diet and you get into the best shape of your life. On the day of the contest you find there are over fifty girls and the room in which you are being judged is not nearly large enough to accommodate all the contestants. That's what happened here. The judges simply did not see my wife."

Georgia added: "I don't know what the judges are looking for anymore. When I am not flexing my muscles I want to look like a woman. I want to have sex appeal. When someone looks at me I want them to say, hey, she's an athletic looking woman. I don't want to go around with knotty muscles all over me. I don't want people thinking right away that I must be some kind of powerlifter."

On the other hand, Georgia wondered whether her height, just under five-feet-eight-inches, might have been her downfall.

"Some people have suggested that because of my height I look very thin," she said. "But that's not true. My thighs measure 22¾ inches, my arms, 12½ and my calves are nearly 13 inches, my chest is 39 inches. I want people to notice me at these contests and now I just don't know what to do."

As far as Georgia's son is concerned, however, too many people notice his mother. And he is embarrassed by that.

"I have had a lot of local publicity back home," Georgia said, "and so many of the kids in school ask him about my training, when I am going to compete, that sort of thing. Well, the other day he simply told them his mother had died."

It made Georgia feel awful and when she asked him why he had told his friends such a terrible thing he said: "I just didn't want them asking me about you anymore."

The whole thing bothers Georgia but she fully intends to going on competing, even though she is determined to do so on her own terms.

"I am very worried when I walk on the beach that people will say, 'Hey, look at her back,' or 'Look at her abdominals.' They won't say look how beautiful her figure is," she complained. "Lately I have noticed I am beginning to get striations across my chest and I have lost two inches off my butt. I am going to be very careful how I train because I really have no desire to be a female Arnold Schwarzenegger."

Lorie Johnston believed Patsy Chapman (background) would be the girl to beat at the Miss Olympia. Both failed to win a place in the contest.

When Rachel McLish says there is no better equipment on the market than that produced by Dyna-Cam, her sponsor, it is difficult to dispute her endorsement. Especially when she offers herself as proof.

The judging panel puts Cammie Lusko through her paces.

Said her husband: "The thing is, we have to decide what the criteria for winning are going to be. You can't have a girl winning today and then not being able to place tomorrow. They keep changing their minds about what the female champion must have . . . they must be more consistent."

Both Georgia and Dick believe female bodybuilding is the fastest growing sport in America today. By Georgia's account there are scores of girls, many of whom train at her *The Rare Breed* gym in St. Petersburg, who are working out only because they want to compete later on.

"Most of these women have boyfriends or husbands who are bodybuilders," said Georgia. "Their men push them on and, when you get down to it, bodybuilding gives them something to work towards . . . together."

"I just wasn't ready for that fantastic reaction," said Auby Paulick, the day after she placed second in the most important contest in female bodybuilding.

She had competed before, in the Miss Michigan Physique, she said, "a nitty-bitty-s-m-a-l-l thing. Which she won.

"There were just seven other girls in that one," Auby said, her eyes sparkling with the excitement of the night before. "Nothing like the Miss Olympia."

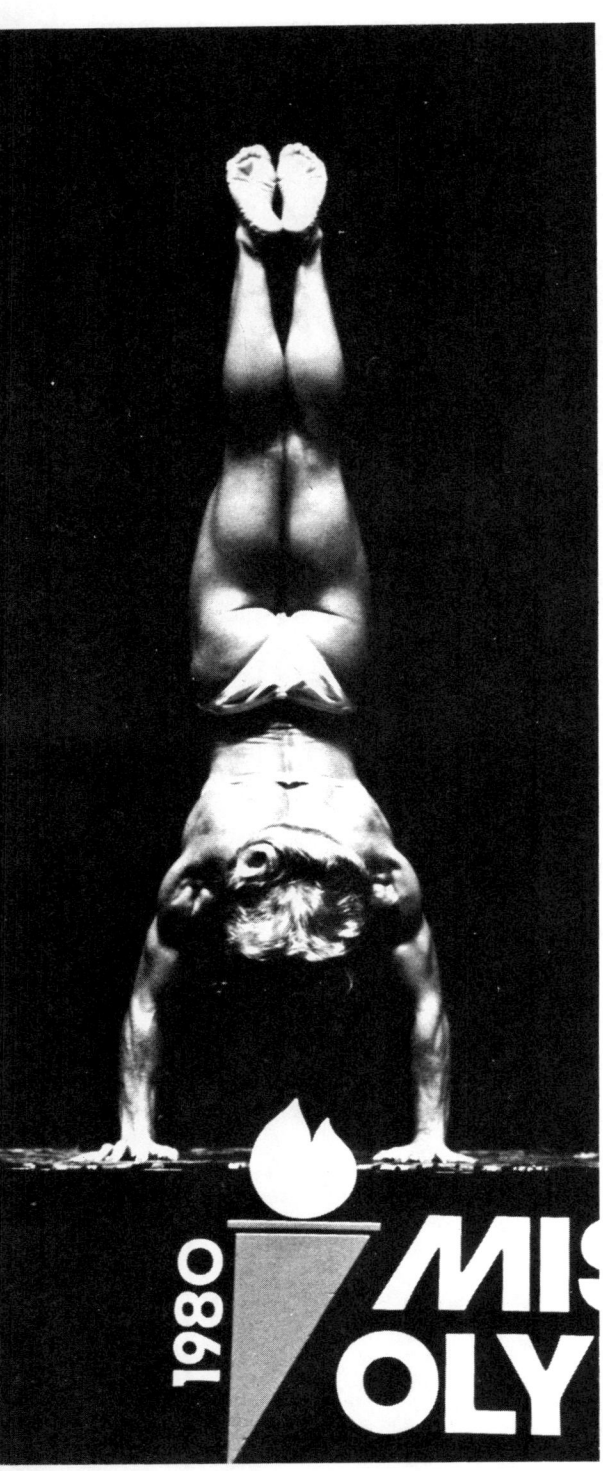

She performed difficult acrobatics . . .

Told that she had appeared very professional in her Miss Olympia presentation, Auby said thanks, she had felt very good onstage and the audience was a great help.

"I have never felt intimidated onstage," she went on, "I love people and I have never been a shy person."

In fact, Auby Paulick works with many people every day. She holds down two teaching jobs: At Troy, Michigan's, Total Fitness Centre and at Gregg's Weight Shop.

"I learned everything I know about bodybuilding at Gregg's," she said. "I train there and I take classes too."

By her account, she had always been a "physical fitness nut." Two years ago, even though she exercised, she noticed a heaviness in her hips and thighs, started developing celluite.

"It was at that point that a friend of mine, a male bodybuilder, suggested I should try weights," she said.

It seemed to be true, as had earlier been pointed out by Georgia Fudge, that behind every female bodybuilder there was a muscleman pushing her on. Auby explained why.

"You see," she said, "Women do not naturally get into weight-training, because they are afraid what their men might say. They worry that they might turn off the guys. So when a guy comes to them and he says, hey, I'd really like you to try this thing, well . . . and when the guy says he'll help out, that's fantastic."

Onstage Auby had performed, among other acrobatic feats, a pressup-to-a-handstand. It is a stunt that few males can duplicate.

"I developed the strength to do this as a consequence of practicing handstand pushups against a wall. I'd kick up to a handstand and allow my feet to rest against the wall. From there I would dip down till my chin touched the floor, then I'd press up again. It was very difficult at first, but then I learned to master it. I performed this exercise for my shoulders. Now I don't need support from the wall or anything else."

As we talked Auby's husband joined us. He trains "very infrequently," would not really call himself a bodybuilder. But he gives his wife all the encouragement he can muster up. Auby is determined to get him training on a regular basis.

I offered the criticism that many of the girls who competed in the Miss Olympia showed a distinct lack of femininity. Auby's husband smiled, as if he was by now a little tired of that barb.

Auby said: "It is so silly to say that. A woman is either feminine or she is not. Bodybuilding won't make her more a woman, nor will it make her less female."

She agreed, however, that some contenders had taken their dieting too far, so that onstage they looked emaciated and sickly.

"You don't have to lose the things that make you look different from a man," she added. "I would be very disturbed if I thought I looked like that. I did not go on a very rigid diet for the Miss Olympia. I merely stopped eating fast foods, cut down on my sugar and so on."

She said she had dropped only about three to four pounds for the contest.

Her husband said Auby was every bit as sensuous as she had ever been, indeed, that it seemed bodybuilding had made her even more sensitive and responsive to him.

Auby didn't care too much for those people who suggested a girl should look one way on the beach and another way for contests.

While George seems more interested in the meat on his plate Arnold Schwarzenegger and Margaret Snyder are captivated by other apparently funny things. That's Joan Fetzer, convention coordinator, looking over George's shoulder.

They came in all shapes and sizes for the Miss Olympia. No wonder the judges had such a difficult time choosing the winner.

She said: "A girl should look her best at all times. I see a girl on the beach and if she is muscular, firm and healthy looking and I am impressed. It's a girl's right to train her body to look the way she wants it. If you ask me whether I think a girl with striations and cut looks grotesque I have to tell you no, not at all."

She said she had had no problems on the beach since she started taking her bodybuilding seriously.

"In truth, I had more whistles and male attention then ever before, Males are much more complimentary about my body these days."

Her husband added: "I think that any man who is at all interested in bodybuilding, for himself or another person, will be tremendously impressed by Auby's development or the development of someone like Auby."

When I asked Auby what it was that had impressed the judges about Rachel McLish to the extent that they had placed the Texan before her, Auby requested a little time to think. Clearly, she had not expected the question, had not even contemplated the possible reasons why she had not herself been declared Miss Olympia 1980.

Brimming with self-confidence a day after her biggest bodybuilding moment, Rachel talks with Rick Wayne about her future.

At last she said, "I don't want to come out sounding like a sore loser, you know? Could I come back to that question later?"

The Paulicks have a stepdaughter, not Auby's offspring, who loves bodybuilding. "She comes to the gym with me," said Auby, "she works out and is totally thrilled with what I am doing."

Suprisingly, Auby never performs situps. Her incredible abdominal development is the result of upper and lower abdominal crunches that she practices every workout.

"Here's how I do them," she said, in her teacher's tone: "I lie on the floor and I practically hypnotize myself into believing that my whole body has become a set of abdominal muscles. I lie on my back, breathe out, then slowly raise my upper body towards my bent knees, as far as I can come up. All the while I am crunching down hard on the abdominal area. It's sort of like a situp with a difference. I get a burning sensation in the area after a few repetitions but I don't stop. Not just then. I go on for a few more repetitions, then I reverse the position. That is, now I bring my legs up towards my head. I keep that up for a few sets. Afterwards, let me tell you, I know I have had an abdominal workout. The exercise also gives me great control of the muscles in the abdominal region."

. . . but finally Auby Paulick was forced to take a back seat to Rachel McLish, the girl from Texas.

I wondered, bearing in mind something that Carolyn Cheshire, a contender from England, had said, whether Auby's husband ever felt threatened by his wife's muscular appearance.

"Not at all," he said. "She's the most beautiful, the sexiest woman that I know. The guy who said he didn't want to make it with a chick who is more muscular than he was displaying his insecurity. I am with Auby all the way. I am never more miserable than when I am overweight so I appreciate the fact that it makes Auby happy to be in shape. And what makes her happy also makes me happy. Our life together is based on physical fitness. We are having tremendous fun with her bodybuilding."

Auby trains three times a week with weights, each session designed to work the whole body, unlike a number of other bodybuilders who train four times weekly, two days for upper body work and two for the rest of the physique. Auby's training sessions last about three hours. She performs her exercises very slowly, employing isometric techniques in a number of the exercises. She does ten to twelve repetitions each movement, always with intense concentration. She prefers incline and decline flyes with dumbbells over barbell bench presses. Because of her very strict training style Auby does not handle the heavy poundages that many female bodybuilders claim they use during workouts.

Finally, we returned to the question that had forced her earlier to ask for time. Now she said, "Everybody wants to win, right? So naturally I was disappointed when the title went to Rachel. I thought we were equally good; she admitted that much to me. But Rachel didn't have abdominal development. Perhaps the judges didn't take that into account when they made their decision. It could have gone either way."

She thought the fact that Rachel had received a lot of publicity in the magazines had helped. She had been asked to send pictures to the magazines, had done so but nothing was ever carried. She was, next to Rachel, an unknown.

"I really don't know why I didn't win last night," Auby said, "I guess I am going to have to ask other people,"

I put one final question to Auby; "Why has women's bodybuilding suddenly become so popular?"

Her husband replied: "People are no longer as ignorant about bodybuilding as they used to be. They know now that bodybuilding need not turn them into a female Schwarzenegger. That they can develop firm, at-

"Had I known the contest would be decided according to those who showed the most muscle," said Kellie Everts, "I would have trained differently." What Kellie has was enough to land her the Miss Nude Universe title in bygone times and much publicity in such magazines as Playboy and Esquire. In the Miss Olympia, however, more was clearly not enough.

Miss Olympia 1980, Rachel McLish. Womanhood in full bloom.

tractive lines and good form while maintaining good health. They know they can look like Auby by training regularly with weights."

There was a time when Kellie Everts, simply by appearing onstage at bodybuilding contests, inspired riotous behaviour. In those days it seemed bodybuilding attention was focused on a slim waist, a generous behind and mammaries that made Anita Eckberg (remember her?) look like an undernourished waif. Yes, Kellie and boobs were as synonymous as rock and dope.

In her time Kellie had stripped for God in a striptease act that was covered by many magazines, more for what she displayed than the words she preached. Kellie had also been Miss Nude Universe and *Esquire* magazine had featured her in glorious flesh color at a time when sales were not nearly as healthy as Miss Everts appeared in her photographs.

Kellie had won a few titles too along the bodybuilding circuit. Lately, however, she had devoted much of her time drawing dirty old men into dimly lit clubs and then entreating them to place themselves in the hands of God.

Kellie entered the Miss Olympia contest looking as she had done for years, which is to say, she had lost none of what she carried fore and aft.

"I had no idea what this contest was about," she said. "I thought it was going to be another one of the competitions, you know, such as I had won before. But I certainly got a surprise."

Indeed, Kellie placed last. She said her coach, who had never trained a woman bodybuilder before, had asked her to build up her bodyweight to 150 pounds but she had refused such advice and instead dieted to 145 pounds. Which was hardly enough a loss to show in the areas that had made Kellie famous. She still looked pretty large.

She smiled a lot under pressure, however. And there was not one single boo from the audience as she went through the same routine that had been seen all over Brooklyn and Manhattan so many times before.

She had nothing to say about the Miss Olympia result. She thought Rachel McLish made a very good winner and regretted very much that she did not know in advance what the criteria for winning would be. She promised to back again, however.

Kellie said it was to be expected, this new trend in female bodybuilding. She said that if muscle and definition were the ingredients for winning that Kyle Neuman and Cammie Lusko should have placed high . . . even though in her opinion they were "bitchy personalities."

She planned to go on with her crusade, that is, stripping for God. And she fully intends to compete again, now that she knows what the judges want to see in a female bodybuilder.

Corrine Machado was Miss Western America in 1979. But all she could manage in the 1980 Miss Olympia contest was fourth place. She and her boyfriend, Brian, run a gym in San Francisco's Bay area but at one time she was an Oral Surgical Assistant. She has been training with weights a little over three years.

I asked Corrine how it felt to place fourth in the Miss Olympia having been number one a short time earlier.

"It doesn't bother me at all," she said. "I know now what I have to do to win and I am going to spend time preparing for the next Miss Olympia."

She had come to think very little of her Miss Western America title because of the criteria by which she had been judged.

"It was a just a beauty contest," she explained, "with emphasis on sex appeal. It really had little to do with training and dieting and so on. The Miss Olympia is the way to go and I will train harder for the title next time."

She said girls had to be careful in training for bodybuilding contests not to get carried away with developing some areas more than others.

"I have seen girls with hardly any chest development showing big muscular legs and thick backs," she said. "If a girl is the small busted type she should be careful not to develop overly muscular arms and thighs. When I train I don't try to copy anyone's figure. I keep check of myself, the way I look. I enter the contest with what I have and then leave it to the judges to decide. But I won't allow any trends to sway my own judgement."

The first time Corrine entered a bodybuilding contest she had been talked into doing so by her boyfriend and his sister. A bodybuilding friend had told her she would be competing and when she mentioned this to Brian and his sister they both got behind her to enter the competition too. She won, even though she was somewhat embarrassed by some of the other entries.

"There were only three of us who actually worked out with weights," she recalled. "I felt almost ashamed to be competing on the same stage as the other girls. I mean, all they did was flaunt their bodies in the sexiest possible

Corrine Machado was once Miss Western America. She placed fourth in the Miss Olympia and swore to return better than ever.

Carolyn Cheshire in action at the Miss Olympia.

way. When I compete I don't present my body as a sex symbol. I think I am participating in an athletic activity and I try to come prepared in every respect."

Brian has his own story about how Corrine first got started. "We had been going out for some time," he said. "At that time I ran a gym in San Leandro and I guess she got tired of always waiting for me to finish work. After a while she started going to the gym with me and soon she began working out herself."

Brian admits that in some cases it looks like bodybuilding has robbed girls of their femininity but he believes such girls were not all that feminine in the first place.

"A girl won't be less a girl just because she has been careful about her diet and exercises with weights," he pointed out. "On the other hand, a girl who has never been all that feminine, when she starts to sprout muscles, will look more than ever like a man. The fact is that it all depends on the individual. If she wants to develop muscles like a man then she certainly can. But I doubt very much that she will ever amount to anything in this sport."

Corrine is careful not to put down those competitors who are extremely muscular. "It's bodybuilding," she says, "and if that's what it takes to win, some girls who want to win badly enough will develop the striations to please the judges."

For her own part, Corrine says she purposely develops as much clear-cut muscularity as possible whenever she is competing. But after the contest she can revert to a less striated figure simply by increasing her food intake.

"The men do it," she said. "They train and follow special rules just for a contest. They develop extreme muscularity for competition but once the contest is over they return to more normal diet and training and soon lose the striations and muscularity. It's the same story with women bodybuilders. I have to say that I personally don't like extreme muscularity on women."

In England muscle girls have never been season, The English apparently like their women softer, curvier and more along the lines of a trained Raquel Welch. So the girls who have won the top titles have never had difficulty making their way into the world of modeling and films. In truth, the girls who compete for Nabba titles are not all that much unconventional. Indeed, they are very much in line with the average male fantasy: Curvy hips, 34 to 36 inch bust and long, firm legs.

A graceful pose of Stacey Bentley.

You won't catch a beauty contestant flexing her latissimus dorsi in the face of a judging panel, no sir. Not even at the annual Miss Bikini contest, run in conjunction with Nabba's Mr. Universe event, will you see a girl flex a bicep. It's just not the done thing, sir.

So where did Carolyn Cheshire get this penchant for biceps and triceps?

"Well," said the 22-year-old the day after she failed to place in the 1980 Miss Olympia, "my boyfriend works out with weights and he always had the magazines at his place. I got interested after reading about the women's contests in America."

Before that, of course, Carolyn had been working out with weights and entering the usual Miss events in British bodybuilding. But now she is definite about the new trend. It's the only way to go, she ways with unbridled enthusiasm.

Carolyn dismisses the suggestion that the enthusiasm displayed at the Olympia is similar to that felt at the better circuses.

Says Suzy Green: "There has got to be a difference in judging female bodybuilders. We are not men and should not be expected to pose like men."

"Nonsense," she said. "I have no doubt that a small percentage think the whole thing is, well, sort of freaky. But by far the majority would love their girlfriends to have legs like Rachel McLish, that they could show off in their shorts. When a female bodybuilder walks in her swimming costume on the beach cuts a beautiful figure. You don't have to be in contest condition every day of your life. People have got to understand that you can do whatever you want with your body and training with weights is the only way to go."

Told about a male champion who said he would have nothing to do with a woman who could out-muscle him, Carolyn smiled her very British smile and said: "Obviously the problem lies not in the girl but in the man who would say something as silly as that. He's got an ego problem that has nothing to do with female bodybuilding."

Carolyn insists the whole thing, female bodybuilding as a sport, requires greater publicity. Some features must be explained, she pointed out. The main gripe is that women lose their bustline and behinds as a consequence of heavy weight-training, as she told it.

"Well, it is simply not true that bodybuilding causes a girl to lose her bust and bum," she said. "Competition today demands that a body be as fat-free as possible. Women are expected to show what muscles they have in their thighs and their backs. Not when we are standing relaxed but when we tense up. If a woman decides to be a competitive bodybuilder at this time then clearly she will have to show what is required for victory. Of course, a fat-free body will have little fat in the bust and bum areas. That's all we have up there and down here anyway. Fat. A contest diet or very intensive workouts will burn fat away. But a woman, if she wants the usual bustline again can simply go back to eating in a way that will fatten her chest out after her contest,"

Carolyn and her boyfriend arranged their vacation specifically so they could take in the Miss Olympia contest. He found the event "Totally exhilarating and can't wait for the next."

Her failure to place did nothing at all to dampen Carolyn's or her boyfriend's enthusiasm for female bodybuilding. She will return to England determined to do all in her power to gain acceptance for her sport. She will compete in the next Miss Bikini but the poses that she plans to offer the judges will be nothing like they have ever seen before.

"I am going to hit them with biceps poses and I will train for more muscularity and size," Carolyn said.

"Well," she replied, "I don't expect to win but someone has got to get the ball rolling and I believe that after a while female bodybuilding as it exists in America will be fully accepted in Britain."

Finally, Carolyn said she preferred the new trend "better than anything that has gone on before."

"This is what bodybuilding is all about," she said. "It has taken physical culture a step further. I train hard, five times a week, and I watch what I eat so that finally I can be judged by what I have achieved. Good symmetry, muscle tone and so on are important to me. I don't want to be just some pretty little face with fluffed up hair and a natural in-and-out figure. This is a sport with its own rules, its own criteria. And that is how the public must look at it."

Although she has been training nearly six years Carolyn says she has never herself taken any form of anabloic steroids. She admits, however, that she has heard a lot about American girls who do.

Kellie Everts may have caught the camera's eye here (extreme left) but she failed to impress the judges. Later she said she had not known in advance what was required of Miss Olympia contenders.

*Carolyn Cheshire
England*

"I have no proof of it," she went on, "but I hear the gossip. I know it would be a very foolish thing to do, for nothing bodybuilding can offer would make up for the side effects that I have read about. Drugs must have no place in a woman bodybuilder's program. They are even more dangerous to women than they are to male athletes. And that's saying a lot."

In London, Carolyn trains at a gym where the majority of the members are men. In fact, she is the only female member. She says she gave up training at a spa because she could not train her arms as she wished with the available equipment. Now that she trains with men, she says, she can push herself harder and she has all the equipment she requires.

How do the men react?

"Well," says Carolyn, I doubt very much they have the time during our sessions to observe that I am a woman. During a workout I am merely another bodybuilder to them. And we encourage each other, help each other achieve our goals."

*Rachel McLish
— Miss Olympia 1980 —*

What They Said

If the majority were disappointed with the result of the Miss Olympia contest, in the eyes of Patsy Chapman nothing showed that might have suggested even a crack in her own self-confidence. Clearly she remained proud of her particular bodybuilding achievements. You got the feeling as you talked with this young woman who only a few months earlier had been adjudged *Best In The World* that a sad day had dawned for female bodybuilding, just when it had appeared to be moving along sane lines.

She said the result of the 1980 Miss Olympia had not surprised her. She had come hoping to win, of course, was aware that many of the other contenders considered her the woman to beat, but after a few minutes at the pre-jugding had come to suspect what the judges were looking for.

I'll wait and see how the sport develops before I decide to compete again," says Patsy Chapman.

"It seems the criteria for winning continues to change," she said. "The contestant has no real idea what is expected of her . . . and pretty soon you realize the judges themselves don't know how to measure us up."

Patsy was reluctant to comment on the girls who had won. It took much persuasion on the part of the writer to get her to speak out. Finally, she said: "The girls were all of a very high caliber, well shaped and all that . . . but personally I don't want to look like . . . well, I don't want to be as muscular as some of them. You hear talk, you hear guys saying a woman was lacking in size here and there, that she needed arms that were more muscular and bigger, stuff like that, and I don't agree. That's not my idea of what a well-developed woman ought to look like. It strikes me as ridiculous for a woman to have muscular 14 inch biceps."

As Patsy told it, it's a novelty when a woman appears onstage with a lot of muscle exposed but quite a different matter when she gets out into the street.

"When you are out there among the public," she went on, "when you have to deal with the looks you get in the

Pre-judging at the 1980 Miss Olympia contest.

street or at school or the office . . . well, it's easy to see the conflict. I feel the winning girl ought to be able to go onstage and impress the judges, then go out on her normal business and feel a part of everything without experiencing negative feelings. The female bodybuilder is quite capable of drawing congratulatory comments from members of the public. It happens all the time. But a girl who is particularly large and muscular, especially when she is about five feet tall, almost always inspires ridicule in the street."

She said she considered a female bodybuilder "overdeveloped" if her muscularity was clearly evident even when she stood relaxed.

"You really don't want to see veins and striations on a woman's body when she is standing there making conversation and not flexing up," Patsy said.

Patsy Chapman began working out with weights while still in high school, five years ago. She got into competitive bodybuilding after reading about the sport in a bodybuilding magazine that a male bodybuilder had given her. Contrary to a number of other cases, Patsy was not pushed into competitive bodybuilding by a boyfriend.

"As I said earlier," she explained, "I had done bodybuilding with a school program and then I had quit. But I always intended to return to training with weights. The magazine simply motivated me to go back sooner that I might otherwise have done."

The near flawless body of Georgia Miller Fudge gives no indication whatever that the lady is the mother of a teenage daughter and son. Miss Olympia or not, Georgia is obviously a winner all the way.

Patsy Chapman also expressed dissatisfaction with the mandatory poses required of female bodybuilding contests. Indeed, her own posing routine had differed from those of the other contenders for the Miss Olympia title. It seemed she had leaned more towards poses that showed good lines, that required grace, while many of the other girls stuck with poses that allowed them to show the most muscularity.

"It is my view that a girl does not have to strike double biceps poses in order to show that her arms are firm. A girl can do a side chest pose without giving the impression she is Robby Robinson or Casey Viator," she said. "You have to be creative."

She trains two hours a day, four to five times weekly. She also practices dance, runs and rides her bike.

Currently Patsy is completing a course in journalism and telecommunications. She hopes later to work with a newspaper.

Her workouts include the usual exercises, from bench presses and flyes to squats and situps. But she does not believe in heavy training. Instead she goes for high repetitions. The most weight she ever used in bench presses, for example, was 95 pounds on a barbell.

She considers her biceps big enough at 12 inches and so avoids all direct arm work. She believes her triceps receive enough growth stimulation from the bench press movement.

"I get enough comment about my arms as it is," she chuckled. "I don't want to make matters worse."

Finally Patsy Chapman said her future in competitive bodybuilding would very much depend on the direction the sport takes in the next few months. She said she had no intention to strive after the extremely muscular look that had proved so successful in the Miss Olympia contest. She said she felt things would change, that the IFBB would finally decide on a formula that would encourage girls to train hard without aiming for a physique that in any way resembled that of Mr. America winners.

"I insist on developing the sort of body that is attractive on the beach, in the street and yet is firm enough and sufficiently shapely to impress bodybuilding audiences and judges," Patsy said. "There is no better way to develop a beautifully shaped body that is strong and shows admirable muscle tone. I will always stick with bodybuilding, but the matter of competition will have to remain with a question mark until I see the new direction. Judges must be better informed. Female bodybuilding does not have to be a freak show."

Robby Robinson and April Nicotra at the Atlantic City Professional Pairs contest in 1980.

Stacey Bentley

If the degree of muscular definition displayed by Rachel McLish reminded of the best in male bodybuilding certainly there was nothing in her manner, her voice or demeanor that was not one hundred percent sensuous female.

One day after her finest bodybuilding moment she was the main attraction at an exhibition that featured ultra modern bodybuilding equipment at the Sheraton Hotel in Philadelphia. The exhibition was all part of the package that the Miss Olympia event had offered patrons. Rachel, it turned out, was the main ingredient in a well thought out drive to sell the Dyna-Cam line.

Months earlier I had, doubtless like thousands of other male bodybuilders, admired Rachel's form from the pages of Joe Weider's magazine. Then she had displayed firm and long shapely legs, tiny waist, lean arms and an irresistible smile. Well, at the Dyna-Cam booth the smile was still as magnetic but somehow it seemed much of the, ah, softness had given way to muscular definition. And I wondered why Rachel had made the change.

She said: "We must not forget that this is supposed to be bodybuilding . . . What we had last night was a bodybuilding contest. A girl has to look like she's been training. My gosh, you can't come out here with a conventionally beautiful figure and that's it. You have to display striations, you've got to show the muscle definition through the skin. It calls for intense training and a rigid diet."

She thought she had won over the other contenders because she had more cuts. "I trained very hard," she went on. "I have cuts in my shoulders that nobody else in the contest had. I was extremely confident and I think that showed through and impressed the judges. I believe that if you can see yourself winning, even in advance of the contest, finally it's going to happen."

She did not buy the criticism that female bodybuilding contests discouraged the feminine look.

"I am not flat chested," she countered, "and furthermore I can tell you bodybuilding enhances femininity. I mean, even though the show is just so sensuous it is also an art, it's very tastefully done and it's beautiful."

She admitted that some of the girls looked masculine but insisted bodybuilding had absolutely nothing to do with that.

"The girls who looked boyish were that way before they ever started working out with weights," she said.

She said she had been training with weights for about five years. However, the intense training that is

Anniqa Fors - Denmark

synonymous with contests had been going on for about ten months. She had gone into competition mainly for the motivation it gives a girl who wants a better physique but might not be all that eager to train under normal circumstances.

She grabbed an opportunity to shout the praises of her sponsor's equipment. "I have trained with all kinds of bodybuilding paraphernalia," she said, "but now I am convinced Dyna-Cam is the only way to go,"

She accepted the fact that there had been some talk, especially from the losers, that suggested she had won the 1980 Miss Olympia because she represented the biggest sponsor.

"Oh," she said, tossing her head back, "sure, I have heard some of the talk but one expects that sort of line from losers. I take it in my stride. My gosh, there's gotta be some sour grapes at contests. To talk like that is to attack the integrity of the judges, who were all respectable and qualified members of the sport."

She did not mind being judged by a panel comprising mainly male judges. She had worried for a little while that they would probable go overboard over the more voluptuous figures at the contest but it soon came to light that they were particularly careful to pick those bodies that showed the result of intensive bodybuilding.

"They wanted to see muscularity," she added. "They kept calling for comparisons."

Auby Paulick

Countering the criticism that female bodybuilders were freakish, Rachel cited Bo Derek and Jane Fonda as examples of female bodybuilding.

"They are very much into training," she said. "If they were to flex up on a stage they would show a lot of muscle. And still you wouldn't say there was anything freaky about Bo."

At 24 Rachel McLish is looking forward to a career in bodybuilding, and not merely as a physique contestant. She is under contract to Dyna-Cam, "because I believe they produce the best training equipment currently available." But more than that the group is spending a fortune promoting their chief apostle. As we spoke Rachel was scheduled to undertake a world tour on *behalf* of Dyna-Cam, soon after she returned from Venezuela with the other Miss Olympia winners. The Venezuela trip was one of the prizes offered by George Snyder.

Interesting enough, Rachel said that one of the conditions in her contract with Dyna-Cam guaranteed her training facilities no matter where she traveled. Naturally, Dyna-Cam gave her no trouble at all in that quarter; the more regular her training the better will the product appear to potential Dyna-Cam clients.

"Bodybuilding is for me an addiction," said Rachel. "I need my fix everyday."

Asked about her personal life in the face of all the publicity her figure had attracted in recent times, Rachel said simply: "I am married." What does her husband think about all that's happening to her? "He just loves it," she said, "he's always telling me to go all the way to the top. He is very supportive."

When not training for competition Rachel works out three times weekly. Her contest preparations demand six training days, however. Each workout takes up about 90 minutes. She does not "go crazy" about diets, eats pretty much what she wants most of the time, "but then I have never been one to eat junk food of any kind." She has never had a weight problem, mainly because she has always been careful about her food, that, plus the fact that she has always been a very active woman.

Clearly Rachel McLish is at the top of the bodybuilding tree. What's more, regardless what the criteria for winning turn out to be she is convinced her place will not be threatened. Yes, Miss Olympia 1980 is a very confident young woman, with no doubts whatever about her worth. She'll be back again to defend her title and with all the ingredients for winning . . . whatever those might be!

The Weider brothers have some fun at Rick Wayne's expense. But wait till Rick gets back to his typewriter.

A New Direction

Three weeks following the 1980 Miss Olympia contest Ben Weider was still uncertain how he felt about the direction that female bodybuilding was taking. He had been hoping for a sign that what had appeared on the bodybuilding horizon at the end of the Miss Olympia contest was not here to stay, that ultimately sanity would prevail.

After all, male bodybuilding had had its ups and downs. There had been the fat beer-bellied strength heroes who gave way to the Saxons and Charles Atlas. There had been that chapter in bodybuilding when body mass was the name of the game, not forgetting that period when bodybuilders appeared in various magazines armed with a pole, their bodies glistening, a strategically placed plastic fig leaf standing between them and the law. Say it straight, bodybuilding had then taken a plunge as it were, from the stages of the leading theaters of the world

Lynn Conkwright

to the pits of insignificance. Indeed, for a long time bodybuilders were offered as freaks at shows that were never meant to enhance the reputation of their sport. People preferred to see well-built men go through their posing routines, so a number of weightlifting promoters used bodybuilders as bait to attract audiences to their weightlifting meets.

And then Ben Weider and his brother had arrived on the scene to restore the sport that clearly had fallen on bad times. It had taken much work on the part of the brothers but gradually they were able to get their message across: Bodybuilding was as much a sport worthy of respect as, say, hockey or football. In time Ben Weider formed the International Federation of Bodybuilders and having traveled the world in behalf of the sport on many occasions, he lived to see his dream come true: Bodybuilding had made prime time television. Bodybuilding was being discussed by intellectuals.

Today, Ben Weider beams with deserved pride when he recalls the bad old days of bodybuilding and his eyes light up as he looks forward to still better times.

Yes, but female bodybuilding was becoming something of a headache for the president of the International Federation of Bodybuilders under whose banner the sport had recently been operating.

He told himself that in the same way that male bodybuilding had developed in time, so the new sport would grow and its rules and direction determined. But Ben could not deny the fact that at each contest a woman more muscular than any he had ever seen before took the top prize. He was pleased that Rachel McLish was attractive, intelligent and in no way masculine. But there were others in the Miss Olympia contest that gave Ben cause to think again.

One week following the Miss Olympia the IFBB president sat open-mouthed at the AAU's Miss America contest. There were a number of very attractive women in the lineup of over fifty contenders but finally the title had gone to a female bodybuilder with fourteen-inch muscular arms and muscular definition comparable to some of the Mr. America aspirants.

Perhaps it was at the moment of Laura Coombs' victory that Ben Weider decided something would have to be done to decide once and for all the direction female bodybuilding would take while it operated under the IFBB colors. We will never know for sure what prompted Ben Weider to set the wheels in motion. Whether it was

The way Arnold told it at the Sheraton, it took a hurricane to get Rick Wayne (extreme right) to leave the Caribbean. Joe and Ben laughed but Hurricane Allen was no joke at all, even if it did blow Rick back to the United States.

the fear that the Laura Coombs' victory would inspire other girls to reach for her proportions . . . and surpass them . . . or something else. No matter, the president of the IFBB now says his federation has taken steps to deter women from using bodybuilding to build male-looking physiques.

"We are all for the enhancing of the natural female form," he has said. "But we will not encourage women to take steroids and diet to the point where their natural female attributes disappear in order to win some small bodybuilding honor."

Ben Weider knows only too well that not all women take steroids to develop muscularity but he has moved in an effort to discourage what is now the winning look, in the hope of discouraging any thought of emulation by those who have not done too well at recent contests.

Patsy Chapman and Rachel McLish were two women that Weider offered as "ideal female bodybuilding examples."

He said he was now conducting a survey the aim of which is to discover how the majority of female bodybuilders feel about their sport. So far, results have clearly indicated that the contenders for bodybuilding titles do not want to look like men, detest the extreme muscularity that currently is so popular at contests.

Lori Snyder and Lorie Johnston during a live television broadcast in New York shortly after the Miss Olympia. Both young women are using bodybuilding as an aid to their individual careers.

"We want the sport to develop along the lines expressed by the majority of its participants," said Weider. "We will over the next few weeks arrive at the various criteria for winning. I can tell you now that while we will look for good muscle tone, we will also expect contenders to display good shape and gracefulness in their posing. Clenched fists and double biceps poses are out. So will the most muscular pose disappear. There has to be a difference in the judging of male and female bodybuilders."

One thing for sure, female bodybuilding is developing rapidly. It is gaining more and more popularity in America and the signs are that London is getting ready to welcome its first female bodybuilding contest.

In April this year Las Vegas will host the Women's Bodybuilding Championships and from advance reports thousands of dollars will be offered the winners. There is also talk of movie contracts and wide television coverage. Ben Weider is set for some proud crowing by the end of

Lorraine Snyder

*While Lorie Johnston goes through her posing routine before the **Livewire** cameras, Lorraine Snyder explains her moves to the show's host. The appearances of the two young women brought in lots of mail from appreciative viewers.*

1981. His federation is determined to do for female bodybuilding at least as much as has been achieved for regular male physique competition.

Doubtless the IFBB president will be pleased to know that the TV moguls are as interested in a shapely and firm female figure as he is himself. Recently Lorie Johnston and Lorraine Snyder appeared on prime time television. The girls also participated in a television show aimed at a young audience. Here they talked at length about the benefits of bodybuilding with weights. Lorraine Snyder is a model and she pointed out that training with weights had been of great use to her career. As for Miss Johnston, herself a contender for last year's Miss Olympia, she posed to music and expertly displayed the figure that weight-training had given her at 18 years of age. The response to this last television program has prompted its producers to invite Miss Snyder and Miss Johnston to perform a second time before their cameras.

The Choice Is Yours

Clearly bodybuilding has come a long way since the early days of Jack LaLanne's studios, when women spent an hour or so three times a week wrapped in the embrace of a vibrating machine that was supposed to help them shed pounds of ugly fat.

Then there were the rollers that overweight ladies sat upon in the hope of remodeling their behinds, to no avail, of course. For it takes a whole lot more than vibrators and rollers to rid the body of unwanted weight: It takes intensive exercise and a sensible diet.

Truth is that the owners of modern health studios have learned a lot more about good business than their predecessors. Whereas the oldtimers took the shortcut and tried to make figure-contouring easy meat for their clients, in the hope that they would enjoy their gossipy sessions at the various health spas and keep renewing their memberships, the modern day gym proprietor is more realistic. He knows that he must show results or his clients will find a more effective way to work off excess body fat, or to gain a few pounds.

Carolyn Cheshire (second from right) is determined to convert her sister bodybuilders in England to the new faith. "I'll flex my biceps and do lat spreads whenever I compete at home," she said. "They might laugh at first but you never know." Indeed.

And so, where the gyms of yesteryear seldom featured useful training equipment the modern gym boasts a variety of machines and an abundance of weights. The client may work her body with dumbbells and barbells ranging in weight from five to one hundred pounds. Or she may choose to train on Nautilus or Universal or Dyna-Cam equipment.

Women who join a gym these enlightened days do so with one thought in mind: To improve their health and figures. And while a great many of them are in their twenties, more and more housewives are turning to weights and away from drugs that supposedly keep the fat off.

Bodybuilding is not the easiest activity in the world. Whether the aim is to maintain a good figure, to lose or gain weight, or to develop the kind of body that wins titles like Miss Olympia, the going can be tough. The wonderful part is that there is a choice. Three to four training sessions a week will be more than enough to give the most out of shape lady an attractive figure in next to no time at all. The weights she will handle in those sessions will depend strictly on her capabilities and what she is trying to achieve.

At Olympus Gym, for example, there are many over-thirty housewives who have developed figures and the looks of twenty-year-olds after training three times a week for less than six months. These people follow very enjoyable training routines involving weight-training exercises that do not over-tax them in the least. They all follow a sensible diet, as recommended by George Snyder himself, and each is given a specific set of exercises. For, while there is no such thing as exercises for the male and female, different people do need different training programs. It all has to do with an individual's requirements. Moreover, some exercises will do one thing for a lady and the exact opposite for another. For example, one lady may have arms that are naturally muscular. It would not be advisable to have such an individual performing heavy barbell curls or exercises that directly promote further growth in the biceps or triceps. Such a person will derive sufficient arm exercise from performing bench presses, standing presses and rows . . . exercises that stimulate growth primarly in the chest, shoulders and back.

Then there are people who do not perform situps because that movement tends to broaden their waistlines. Instead they might do knee raises or perhaps abdominal crunches on the floor.

Those ladies who train with an eye on bodybuilding titles are altogether different cup of tea, however. Because competition is stiff, these ladies, like their male counterparts, must be prepared to spend more time working out. They must develop the determination to succeed, no matter what, at their sport. Those who compete, people like April Nicotra and Lorie Johnston, winners like Georgia Fudge and Rachel McLish, very seldom miss a training session. Sometimes these people will train twice a day, depending on their needs and the time available to them.

Of course, competitive female bodybuilders train with far greater intensity than the ladies who merely wish to rejuvenate or maintain their body lines.

The exercises that make up the various training programs for women are in many instances similar to those employed by male bodybuilders. Which is not to say the exercises will automatically turn a female figure into a male physique; neither can they turn a male physique into something better suited to a lady. As has been pointed out elsewhere in this book, exercise even when heavy

"I really don't know what the judges are looking for anymore," said Georgia Fudge after the Miss Olympia. Certainly it would seem Georgia has all anyone might ask for.

April Nicotra

Lynn Conkwright

weights are employed, do not interfere with a woman's femininity. Moreover, it is not necessarily true that weights can develop very large muscles for a woman. In normal circumstances a woman's hormones simply will not allow her to grow muscles bordering on the dimensions of the male. That's an irrefutable fact. However, a woman may develop muscular definition as clearcut as a Mr. America winner . . . if she chooses to diet specifically for that purpose, or if she is desperate enough to turn to drugs as a means of reaching her goal. Because Ben Weider and the International Federation of Bodybuilders wish to discourage women from developing physiques that to a large extent resemble those of the male, strong steps are currently being taken to de-emphasize the look of extreme muscularity in women. Henceforth, competitive female bodybuilders will be expected to show a balance of muscularity and female form: That is to say, the ladies will be expected to look firm but not at the expense of other factors normally associated with female health and beauty. It is hoped that by strictly controlling the criteria for winning a female ideal synonymous with weight-training and sensible dieting will emerge. As Ben Weider recently put it: "Our aim is to enhance the female body via sensible weight-training; not to develop a new sex that resembles Arnold Schwarzenegger."

And so it seems that while the voluptuous figure may have a pretty difficult time on the female bodybuilding circuit, mainly because such figures have so much fatty tissue in the wrong places, the extremely muscular lady may well be forced to gain a pound or two in the interest of preserving the conventional female shape. Good, we say!

However, the good news is that freedom of choice will be maintained. Those ladies who want to build figures that are extremely muscular may do so anyway, simply by drastically cutting down on calories when the look is required. And they remain free to train with greater and greater intensity in pursuit of the cut appearance. They may not win the top titles in the future but then what is a title compared to your freedom to look as you wish? Interesting enough, the vast majority of female bodybuilders have let it be known that they would welcome any move on the part of the IFBB to play down the muscular look for women. Moreover, they want the federation to take another look at the mandatory poses and to encourage female contenders to steer away from

Lorie Johnston

those postures used by male bodybuilders to show biceps development, muscular pectorals and so on.

In the last chapter are a number of exercises performed by female bodybuilders at George Snyder's Olympus Gym. The exercises are demonstrated by Lorie Johnston, Lorraine Snyder and April Nicotra, who very often workout as partners. In addition to explaining the movements and what they achieve we will offer two training programs, one for the competitive bodybuilder and the other for regular maintenance of the figure. We wish to state at this point that no person should embark on an intensive weight-training program who is in any way suffering physical injury to any part of her body. Indeed, we recommend that before embarking on any program of physical exercise the individual should check her condition with a physician. Having received the all clear signal, the training routines later offered may be approached with full confidence.

Planning Your Training Routine

The whole point to training at a gym is this: Not only is there a wide variety of modern training equipment available you will also have the services of a properly trained instructor; who will be able to correctly analyze your potential and map out routines that will correct what flaws there might be in your figure.

Your training instructor should always monitor the progress you should be making. He should be ever watchful of the effect a particular exercise, or group of exercises, is having on your physique. This is particularly important where the trainee is a beginner. Which is not to say experienced bodybuilders do not require the advice of a good instructor. There really is nothing quite like constructive criticism, and that is where the experienced trainee will benefit most from an "educated" instructor.

Lorie Johnston, Lori Snyder and April Nicotra give television audiences in Philadelphia some idea of their rigorous workout. Miss Snyder is making a name for herself as a model, having produced her own book on figure contouring, **Body Magic.**

Patsy Chapman is, away from the posing platform, a student of journalism and telecommunications.

For example, some exercises will have different effect on different bodies. Some ladies have discovered that the barbell bench press, far from enhancing their bustlines, has a reverse effect on the bodypart. It is the same with many male bodybuilders. Barbell bench presses do very little, if anything at all, for their pectoral muscles. Well, such people would do better from pec-dec squeezes and bent arm flyes.

Then there are people for whom regular situps are a curse. They do the exercise and are horrified to discover their waistlines have grown larger as a result. At the Olympus Gym such trainees have rectified the problem by performing leg raises on a bench or from a chinning bar. Twists also work wonders too.

The trainee should be careful not to over-develop a particular muscle group. For instance, there are young women who have naturally broad backs. Such people should not spend too much time on the lat machine, for obvious reasons. A particularly wide back is not normally a sought after look among women, not even among those who compete for titles. A woman with a very wide back, like Patsy Chapman's for instance, would do better to concentrate on exercises that build muscularity in the centre of the back, without adding the impression of width.

Again, as Patsy Chapman has said, she avoids direct biceps work because already her upper arms are big enough. She is now of the view that such exercises as the bent over row and bench presses are sufficient for the maintenance of her firm triceps and biceps.

And so, in planning a routine the sensible girl will first take a good honest look at herself. She will note where her flaws lie and where she is particularly fortunate. Then she will plan a routine that, while maintaining her good areas, will also correct the imperfections in her build.

The matter of poundages is best left to the individual. Let your guide be the number of repetitions that you can correctly perform in a given exercise. Strength training is altogether a different subject, one that we are not at this time concerned with. Which is not to say the bodybuilder should be reluctant to build strength. Indeed, we will go so far as to say that the minute you discover you are able to do 10 repetitions for four sets of any exercise without too much effort you should increase your training poundage. But don't allow yourself to fall into sloppy training. Most male champions have discovered that particularly

*Rachel McLish and Frank Zane
Miss Olympia — Mr. Olympia*

heavy weights do little for muscle development; that the weights go up and down mainly from the help received from areas that they did not intend to exercise at the time. For instance, say you were curling a barbell, an exercise that is meant to affect mainly the biceps. Well, if the weight you have chosen is too heavy you will find yourself swinging the bar and even though you manage to get the barbell up to the shoulders much of the work in getting it there will have been done by your lower back. Choose your training poundages carefully, good advice for beginner and champion alike.

On sets: It is our view that for most advanced people four to six sets per exercise will be sufficient, we also recommend just two to three exercises, four at the most, per bodypart. Thighs are the exception and most girls will have to double the exercises for this area.

It is up to the individual how often she trains. Those who have the time might want to train six days a week on split routines. That is, on Mondays, Wednesdays and Fridays a woman might wish to train certain body areas, and the rest on Tuesdays, Thursdays and Saturdays. Some have chosen to train in much the same was as male champions, something we do not fault if the lady is herself a very experienced bodybuilder.

Suzy Green

Diet: Now here's a subject that will depend on the individual. Most experienced bodybuilders prefer white meat, however, over red. They enjoy chicken, fish and eggs. They eat lots of fruit when not training for a competition and vegetables too. Most take only very small amounts of milk, cheese and other dairy products. They all watch their sugar intake and keep that to the barest minimum. Many of the lady champions we talked with said they ate about 30 grams of carbohydrates a day; all of them took food supplements, including vitamins and minerals.

The following is a sample of a routine used by some of the leading female champions of bodybuilding. It is a six day program and very advanced. Definitely, it is not for beginners.

Monday- Wednesday-Friday
Abdominals, Chest, Legs, Calves

ABDOMINALS

Crunches: 4-5 sets of 20 reps
Twists: 4-5 sets of 100 reps
Leg raises: 4-5 sets of 20 reps

CHEST

Bench Press: 4 sets of 12 reps
Flyes: 5 sets of 10-12 reps
Incline barbell press: 4 sets of 8-12 reps
Pullovers: 4 sets of 10-12 reps

LEGS

Squats: 4 sets of 20 reps
Lunges with barbell: 4 sets of 20 reps each leg
Leg curls: 3 sets of 15-20 reps
Leg extensions: 3 sets of 20 reps
Leg press: 3 sets of 15-20 reps
Deadlifts: 3 sets of 15-20 reps
Inner thigh machine: 3 sets of 15-20 reps
Outer thigh machine: 3 sets of 15-20 reps

CALVES

Standing calf machine: 3-4 sets of 20 reps
Seated calf raises: 3-4 sets of 20 reps
Lying calf raises: 3-4 sets of 20 reps

Rachel McLish and George Snyder backstage after the Miss Olympia contest.

**Tuesday-Thursday-Saturday
Abdominals, Shoulders, Back, Arms, Thighs**

ABDOMINALS

Repeat Monday, Wednesday, Friday routine

SHOULDERS

Standing laterals: 3 sets of 10 reps
Upright rows: 3 sets of 10 reps
Rear laterals: 3sets of 10 reps

BACK

Pulldowns: 3-4 sets of 8-12 reps
Pulley rows: 3-4 sets of 8-12 reps
Hyper-Extensions: 3 sets 8-12 reps

ARMS

Pressdowns: 3 sets of 8-12 reps
One Arm Extensions: 3 sets of 8-12 reps
Incline curls: 3 sets of 8-12 reps

THIGHS

Lunges w/o weight: 4 sets of 20 reps each leg
Side kicks: 4 sets of 20 reps each leg
Back kicks: 4 sets of 20 reps each leg

Auby Paulick

The lady who does not wish to enter contests might prefer to train three times a week. Certainly that would be adequate for developing and maintaining a good figure.

Mondays-Wednesdays-Fridays

ABDOMINALS

Leg raises on a bench: 3-4 sets of as many reps as possible per set
Sit-ups on floor: 3-4 sets of as many reps as possible per set

CHEST

Barbell bench press: 4 sets of 8-10 reps
Incline Flyes: 3 sets of 10 reps
Pullovers: 3 sets of 12 reps

LEGS

Leg extension: 3 sets of 15 reps
Leg press: 3 sets of 15 reps
Leg curls: 3 sets of 15 reps
Lunges: 3 sets of 15 reps
Deadlifts: 3 sets of 15 reps
Side kicks or outer thigh machine: 3 sets of 15 reps
Inner thigh machine (if available): 3 sets of 15 reps
Back kicks: 3 sets of 15 reps

BACK

Pulldowns: 3 sets of 10 reps
Cable rows: 3 sets of 10 reps

ARMS

Tricep pressdown: 3-4 sets of 15 reps

SHOULDERS

Standing laterals: 3-4 sets of 10 reps

CALVES

Standing heel raises: 3-4 sets of 12-15 reps

The above routine is basically geared for those women who are close to their desired bodyweight. Thin women should eliminate some exercises plus keep their repetitions slightly lower. Heavy women should consequently increase repetitions and, if needed, add exercises to those body parts requiring more attention.

Lorie Johnston poses for New York TV.

Of course, the exercises may be split up into a four-day routine, For example, you may wish to train only your thighs, calves and chest one day, the rest on the next day and so on. the amount of weight used should depend on your ability to correctly perform your repetitions. The gym is no place for gossip and that should be saved for after workout hours if your time at the weights is to prove fruitful.

Stay in touch with your instructor. Let him know how you are making out with your particular program and give him an opportunity to make changes if necessary. As we have stated earlier, the above program is merely a guide. You may pick any exercises from those offered in making up your own routine. Be sure to check the following pages for proper performance of the exercises.

One last hint: We have discovered at the Olympus Gyms that women do best who train their legs as regularly and with the same intensity usually reserved for their waist and abdominals. Women tend to gather fat around the hips, buttocks and thighs much more than men. It's a natural thing for the female of the species. So unless that fatty deposit is closely monitored trouble could arise in the previously mentioned areas. We are not for one minute suggesting there should be no fat on the hips. On the contrary, what we are suggesting is that the female bodybuilder watch her lower body with the same hawkeye that she monitors her waistline. Aim for a rounded derriere; in fact, squats will build attractive and firm glutes. But do not allow too much fat to stick to the upper thighs and buttocks, whatever you do!

April Nicotra and Lorie Johnston lend a hand during a workout at the Olympus Gym in Warrington, Pa. Lori Snyder, center, is George Snyder's daughter.

FOR THE CHEST

Bench press: For some this is perhaps the best chest exercise in the book. A barbell may be used (as illustrated) or the trainee may prefer dumbbells. For beginners, a barbell will serve better because it is easier to handle. Later, when the trainee has gained greater control and is stronger, she may turn to dumbbells. The barbell can be taken off racks or it may be handed to the trainee. Take a shoulder width grip, breathe in deeply, then slowly lower the weight until the bar is barely touching your chest. Now press back to starting position, breathing out at the same time. When dumbbells are used the same method of application is used. This is a good movement for firming up the pectorals, which form the base on which the fatty tissue of the breast stands. The exercise also has good effect on the triceps, helps rid the upper arms of fat, and firms up the shoulders. The number of sets and reps to be performed will depend on the experience of the trainee.

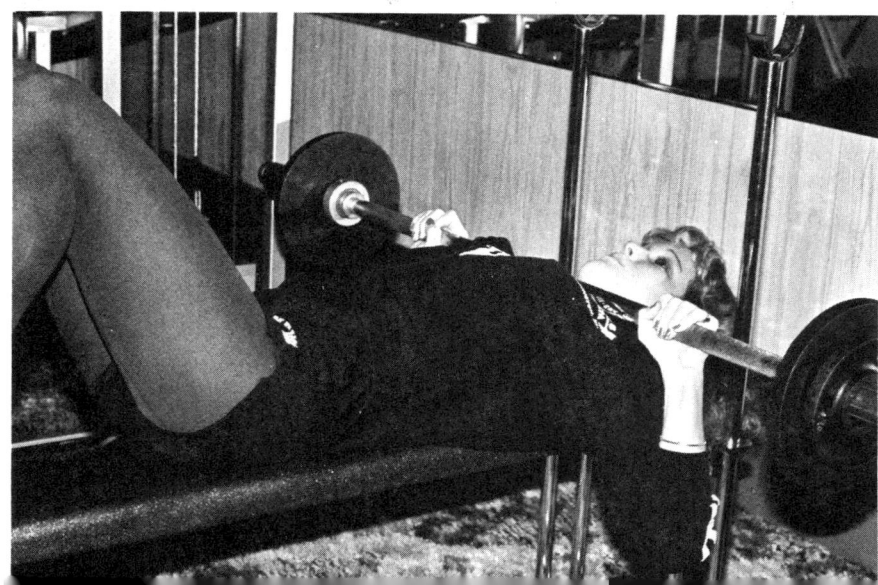

FOR THE CHEST

Incline bench press: Except that an incline bench is used in this version, the exercise is similar to the previous mentioned. In this version there is greater stress on the upper portion of the pectorals. It also places much resistance on the triceps and shoulder muscles. It is a good idea to stay clear of this movement until after about three weeks of using the flat bench version. In our picture Lorie Johnston is using a special incline press machine, which makes it much easier to perform the exercise without losing control. Note that the bar is brought down to a point just below the neck before Lorie presses it back to arms length.

FOR THE CHEST

Flyes: Again there are two versions of this movement, one performed on a flat bench, the other on an incline bench. Both versions are wonderful for toning up the pectorals and developing a bustline that is firm and attractive. Begin with the dumbbells held at arms length over the chest. Breathe in, then slowly lower sideways as low as you can comfortably go. Return to starting position, then breathe out. Repeat until the required number of reps have been done. Note elbows are slightly bent to eliminate undue stress on the elbows.

FOR THE CHEST

Straight arm pullovers: This exercise is great for stretching the entire ribcage and building up the higher area of the bust. Start with the weight held at arms length, as illustrated. Breathe in deeply, then lower as far back as possible. Now breathe out as you return to starting position. Feet should be on the bench so that the ribcage is not held tight by surrounding muscle and is therefore more amenable to stretching.

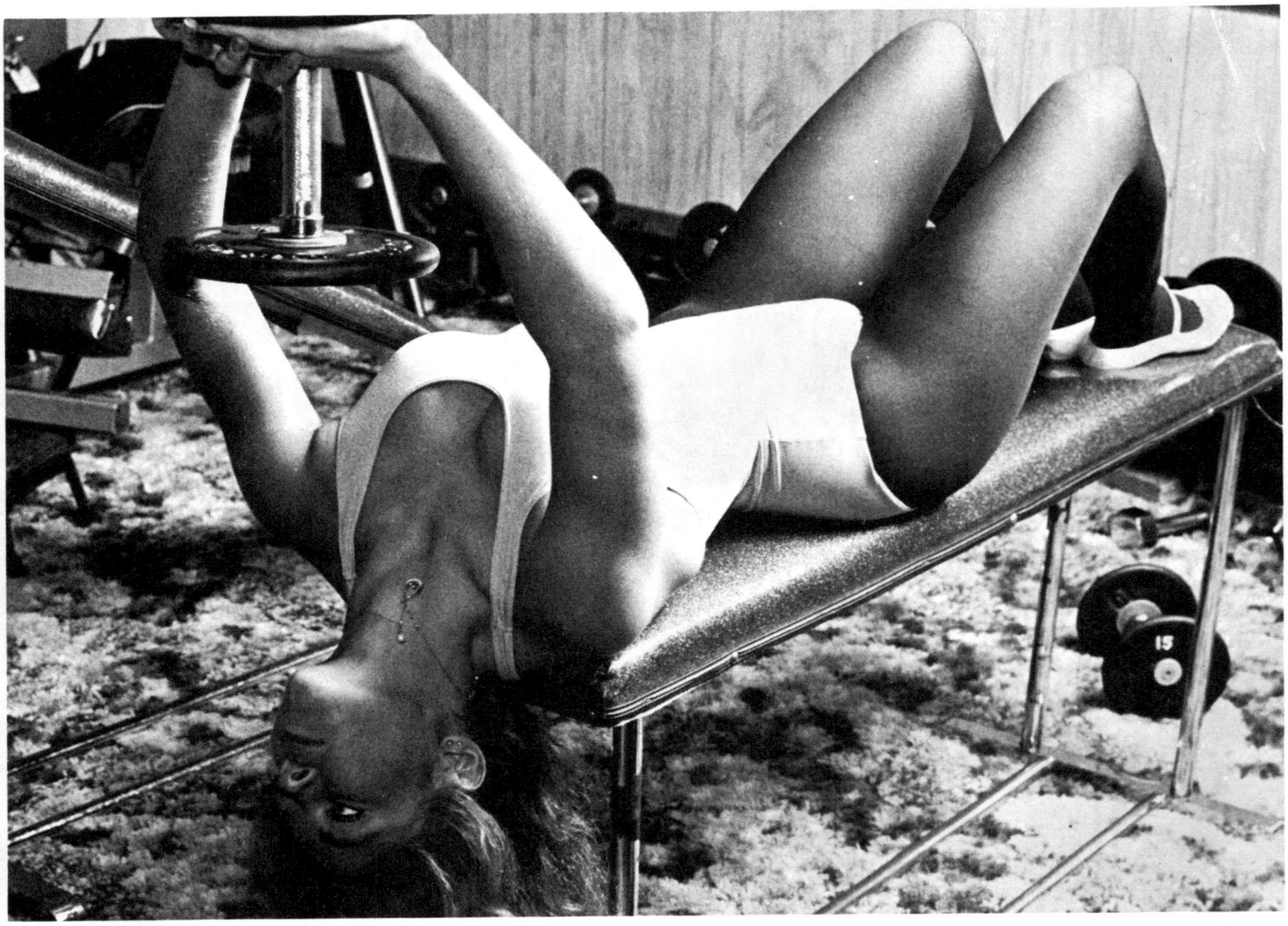

FOR THE CHEST

Pec-Dec Squeeze: The equipment used here is fairly new but is to be found at most reputable gyms around the country. Begin the movement with the handles firmly gripped and at the front of the body. Now breathe in deeply, then slowly bring the arms back as in the second picture. From here forcibly return to starting position, The exercise is wonderful for toning up the whole bust area and developing a higher chest.

FOR THE CHEST

Cable Crossovers: Again this is standard gym equipment these days. Note starting position. Bring the arms down until they cross at the wrists. Concentrate strongly on the effect of the exercise on your pectorals, the muscles beneath your breast tissue. Breathe out as you bring your arms down, then breathe in and return to starting position. Repeat. This exercise can also be performed one arm at a time, thereby allowing some trainees better concentration for a more effective movement.

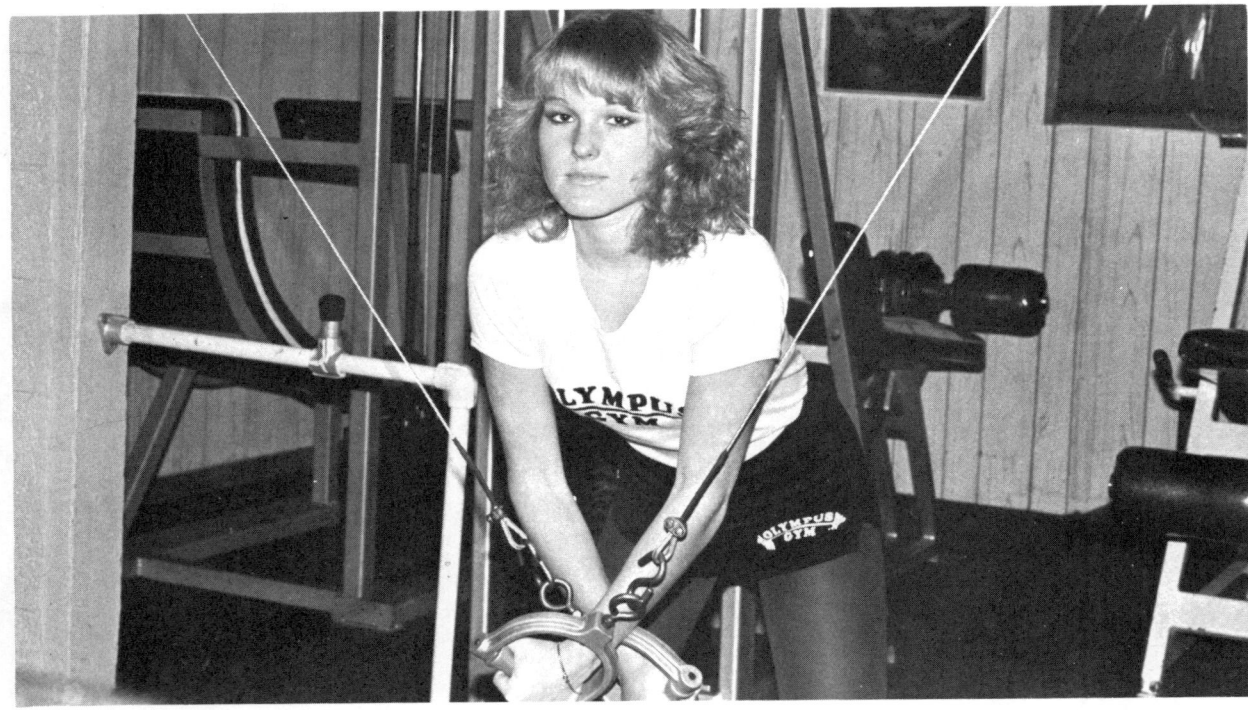

FOR THE CHEST

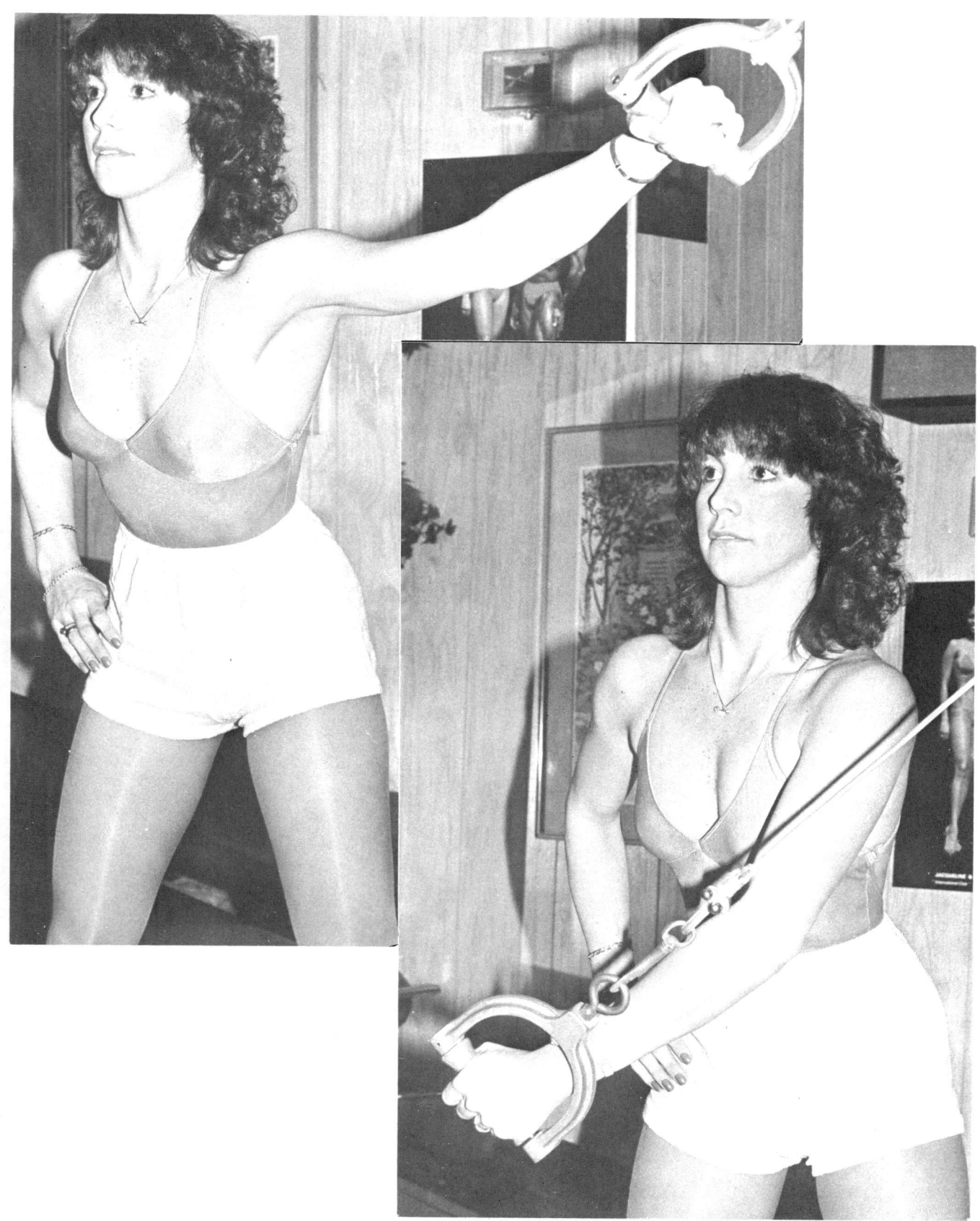

FOR THE BACK

Lat pulldowns: Take up the position illustrated by Lorie Johnston at the lat machine. From here, breathe in deeply and at the same time pull the bar down till it touches the back of your neck. Now slowly return to starting position and exhale. Repeat. It is important that you use a weight that will allow you to perform the exercise properly for the required repetitions. This is great for firming up the upper back muscles and improving posture. For variety, the bar may be pulled to the front. Do both versions for best results.

FOR THE BACK

Cable rows: Wonderful for building attractive muscle in the center of the back. It is also most effective as an exercise for toning up the biceps of the upper arms. Adopt position illustrated by Lori Snyder. Now pull the handles to your waist, making every effort to keep the back straight throughout. Breathe in as you pull and out as you slowly return to starting position. Try to reach forward as far as possible on the return.

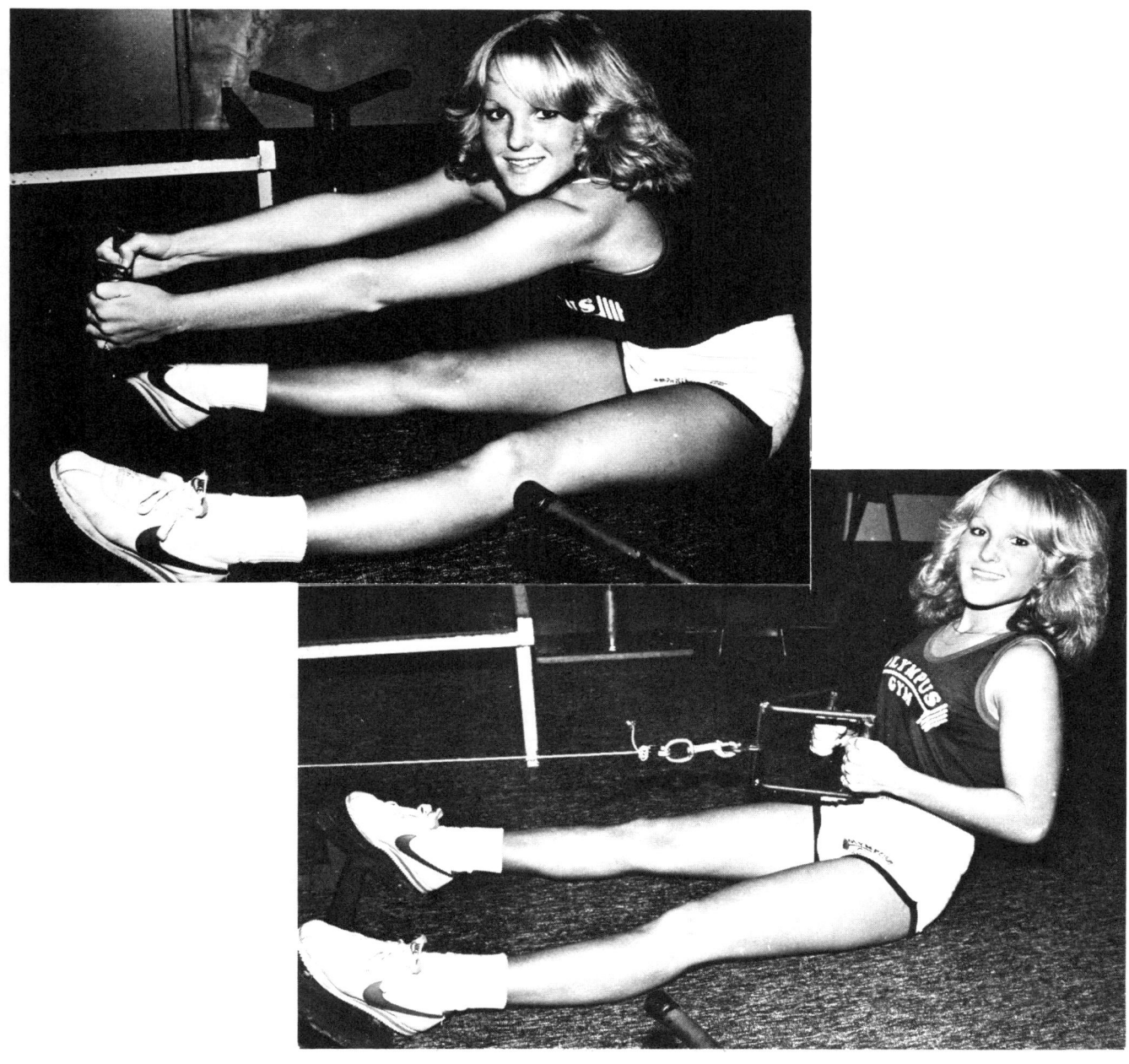

FOR THE BACK

One arm dumbbell rows: are primarily for widening the back. The exercise also has good effect on the shoulders and upper arms. Note the starting position, with feet apart, knees bent and free arm resting on a bench for support. From here the weight is pulled as illustrated to the chest, then slowly lowered again. Breathe in as the dumbbell comes up and out as you lower. Having done the required amount of reps with one arm, change over to the other. Take a rest when you have done the exercise with both arms.

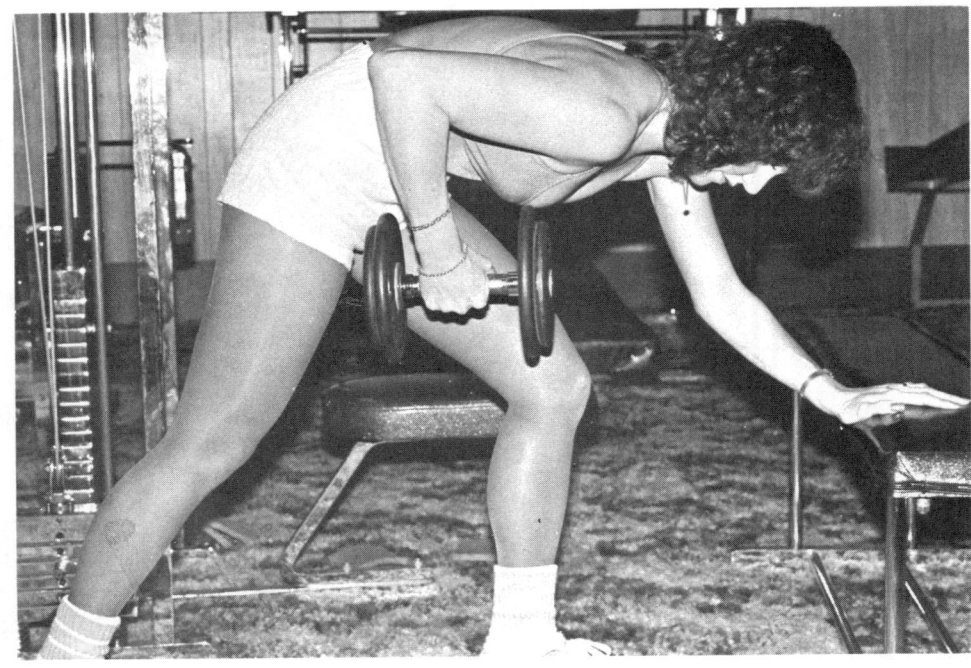

FOR THE BACK

Hyper extensions: will work miracles for the lower back, an area where women are prone to develop rolls of ugly fat. Place your hands at the back of your neck as shown by Lorie Johnston, feet held down. Now let your upper body go down as low as possible, and slowly. Having reached lowest point, return vigorously to starting position. In our picture Lorie is using gym equipment but the exercise can be done on an ordinary exercise bench with a partner holding your feet down. We recommend that you breathe out as you go down, then in deeply as you rise again. Try to work up a rhythmic action throughout the exercise.

FOR THE SHOULDERS

Upright rows strengthen the upper back and are great for toning up the shoulder area. Grip the barbell as shown, breathe in, then raise the weight till the bar is at a point just below your chin. Try to keep your elbows pointing upwards. Lower slowly and breathe out. do not swing the weight. Instead try for a smooth movement up and down.

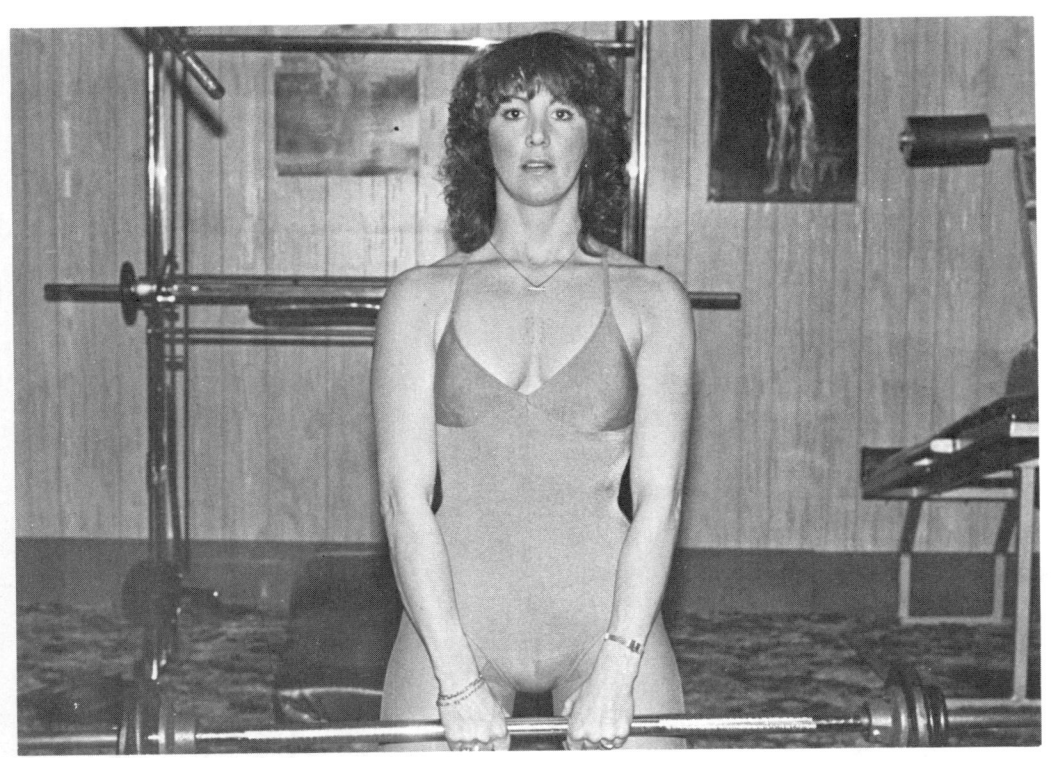

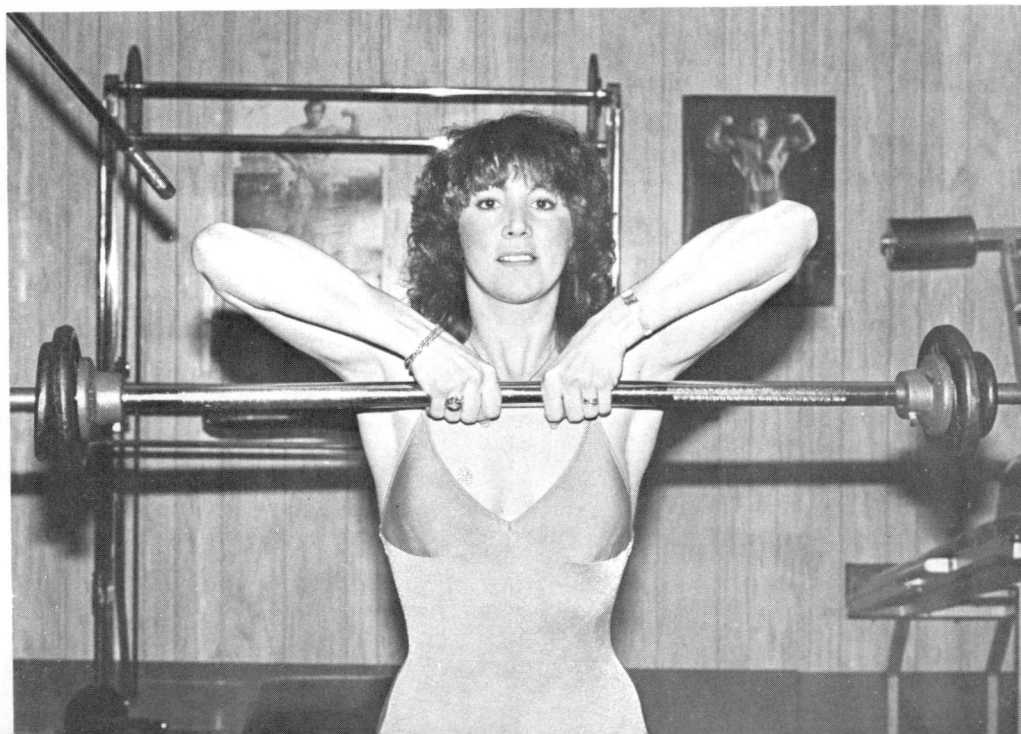

FOR THE SHOULDERS

Seated presses are best done on the machine pictured here. Take up the illustrated position with feet firmly planted on the floor. Now breathe out and push the handles up to arms length. Lower as you breathe in. Repeat. Start with a poundage that will allow you to do 10 repetitions.

FOR THE SHOULDERS

Standing laterals serve to define the deltoid muscles that cap the upper arms. Adopt the starting position, weights held in both hands at the front of your thighs. Now breathe in and raise the dumbbells sideways to a point parallel with your ears. Do not swing the dumbbells. Use a weight that will allow you to raise your arms mainly with the strength of your deltoid muscles. Breathe out as you lower.

FOR THE SHOULDERS

Rear laterals affect the posterior portion of the deltoid muscles. Again the pec-dec machine is used but the position is now reversed. Instead of sitting with your back against the machine, as you did when the purpose was to work your chest, you position yourself as illustrated by Lorie. Grab the machine handles and slowly bring both arms back as far as possible. Breathe in as your arms travel backwards and out on the return. The exercise is also great for strengthening the upper back.

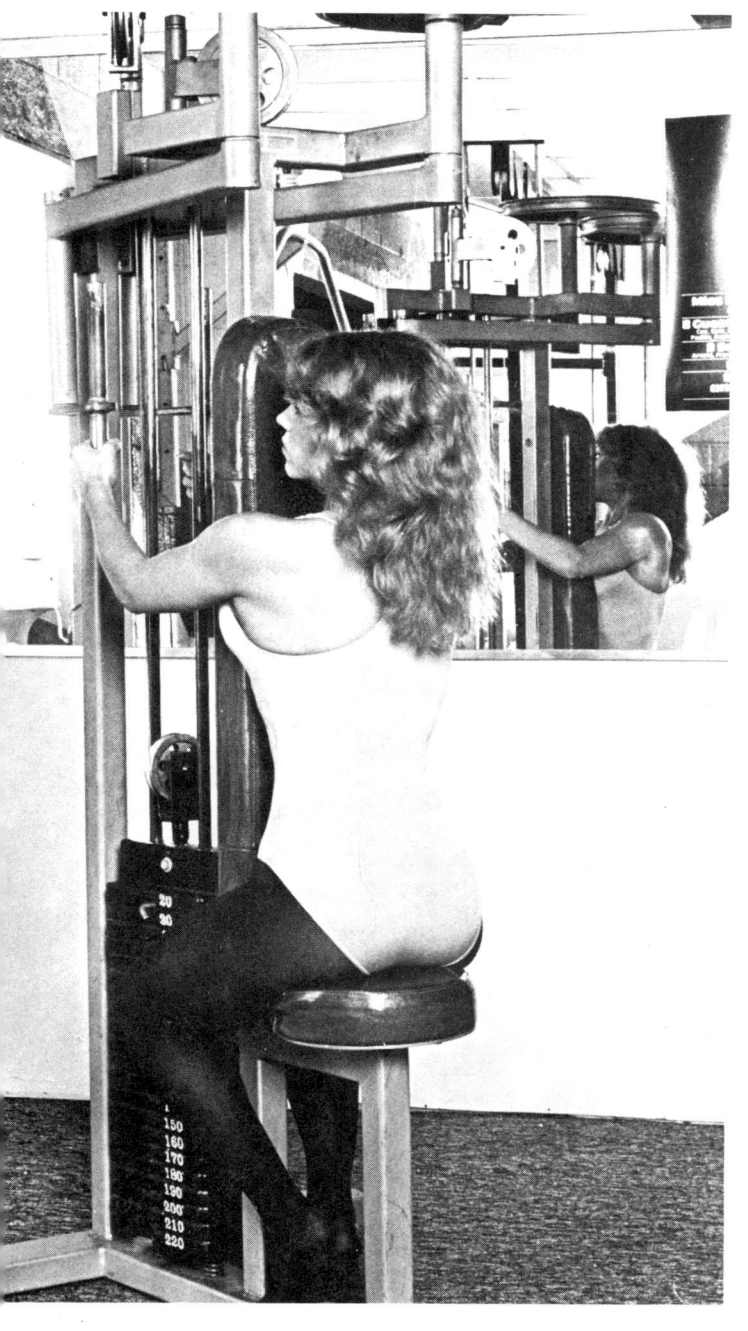 

FOR THE SHOULDERS

Rear laterals with dumbbells is another variation of the posterior deltoid movement. Sit at the end of an exercise bench, feet firmly planted on the floor. Now pick up a pair of light dumbbells, breathe in and, still in the bent over position, raise the weights to shoulder level. Do not swing the dumbbells. Breathe out as you lower the weights behind your legs. Study illustrations.

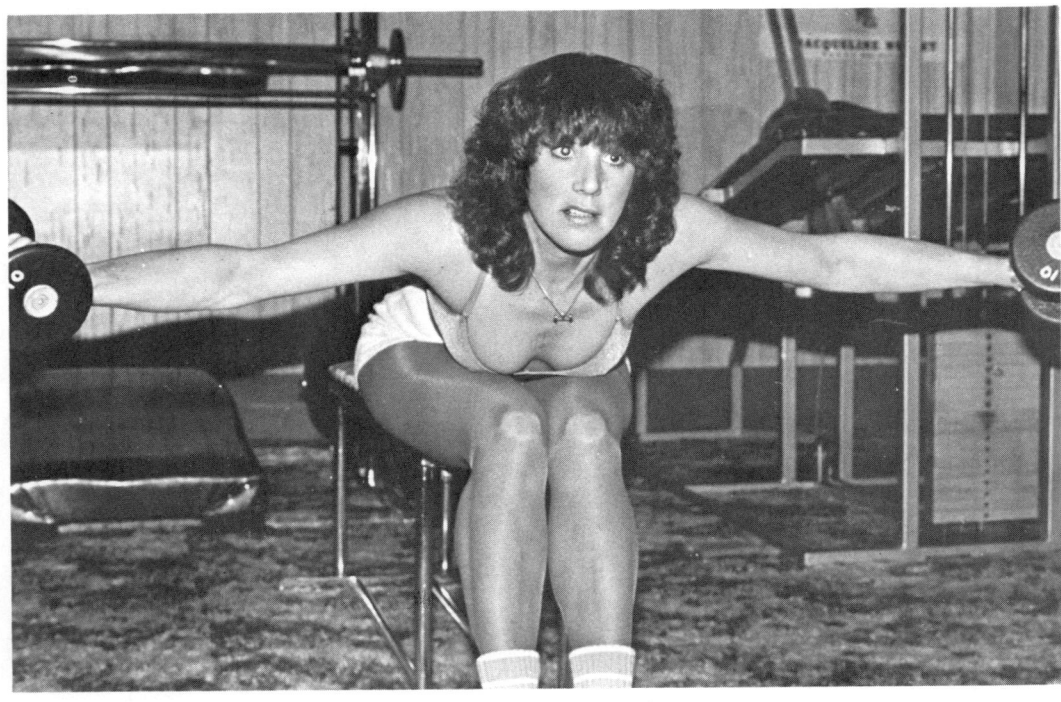

FOR THE ARMS

One arm triceps extension: Begin with a dumbbell as shown. From the starting position, and with elbow pointing upwards, slowly lower the weight to the back of the neck as low as you can go. Then return to starting position. Thought by many to be one of the best exercises for the triceps.

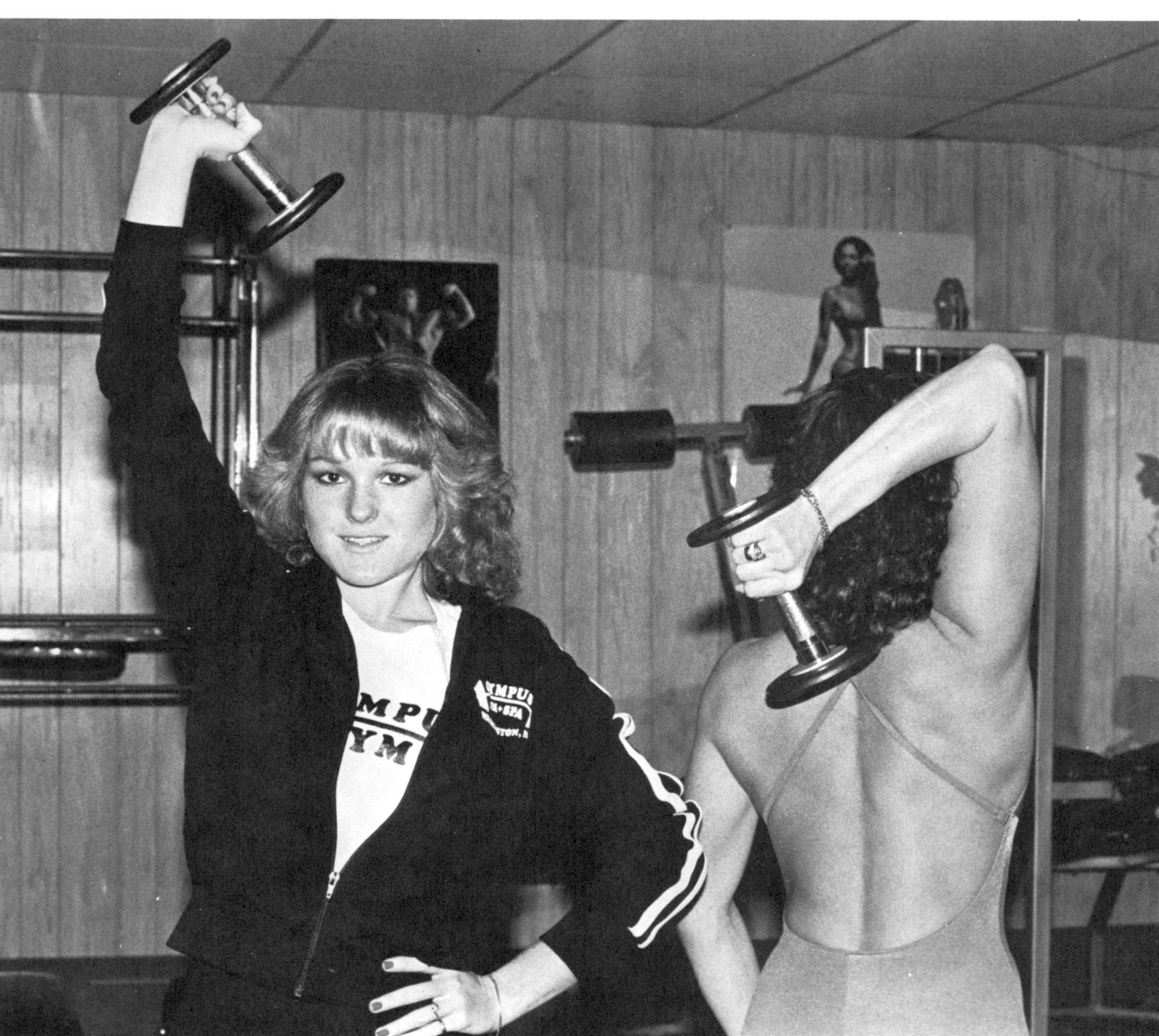

FOR THE ARMS

Pressdowns on the lat machine will firm up and define your triceps. Face the machine while holding the handgrip in both hands. Try to keep upper arms close to your sides as shown. Now, with the upper arms still in position press down with your hands until the arms are straight. Hold for a count of two then slowly return to starting position again. Do not allow elbows to move sideways. Great for working off ugly fat at the back of the arms.

FOR THE ARMS

Reverse dips again work the triceps vigorously. Adopt starting position as illustrated. Now slowly drop your body downwards as low as possible, placing as much resistance on your triceps as you can. Then press up back to starting position. Try to use as much triceps strength as possible, and endeavor not to cheat by deliberately raising your buttocks. Press your body back to starting position with arm strength mainly.

FOR THE ARMS

Barbell curl: This is a basic biceps exercise, one that enjoys great popularity because it allows the trainee to use considerable weight. It can build size in the biceps as no other movement can. Hold a barbell in the position shown, palms facing forward, then slowly curl the weight up to your shoulders. Lower slowly and repeat. Breathe in as the weight is lifted and out on the downward phase. Do not swing the barbell.

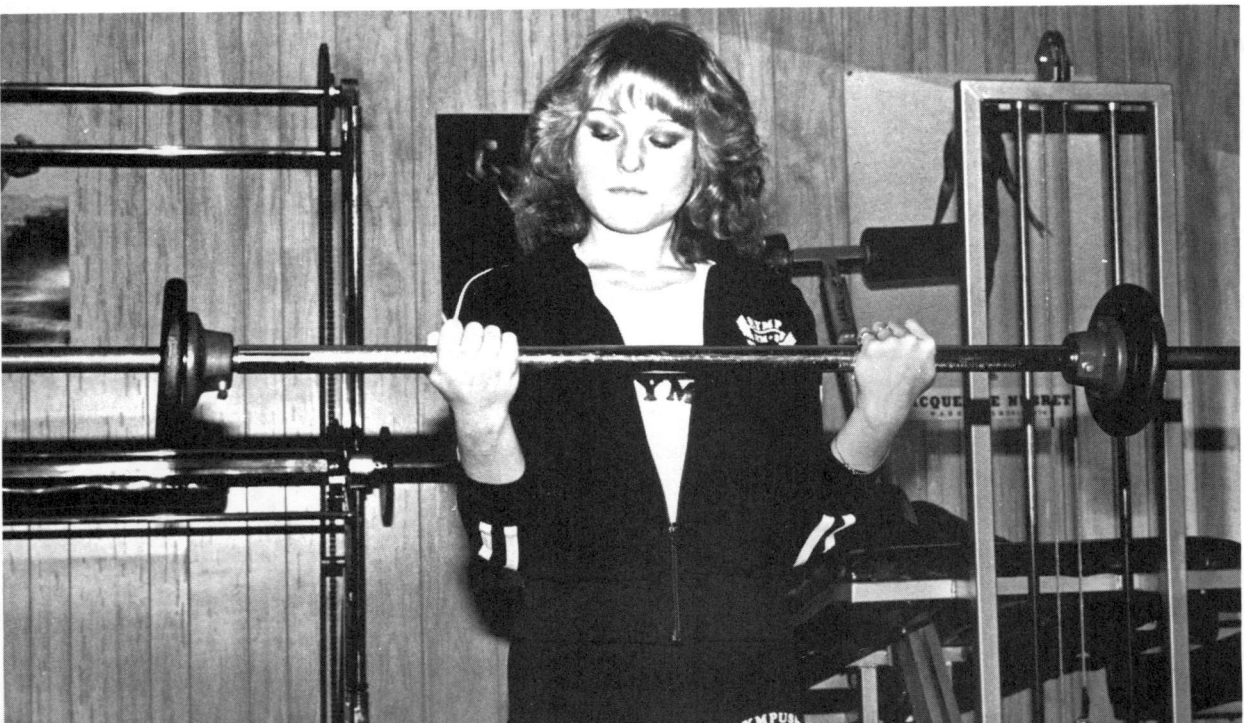

FOR THE ARMS

Incline curls with dumbbells are great for lengthening the biceps muscle, giving it good shape and working its outer head. Use a 45 degree angle for best results. Let the weights hang down as low as possible at the start of the movement, then breathe in deeply as you curl the dumbbells up to your shoulders. Lower and breathe out. do not drop the weights on the return. Instead, try to lower them slowly.

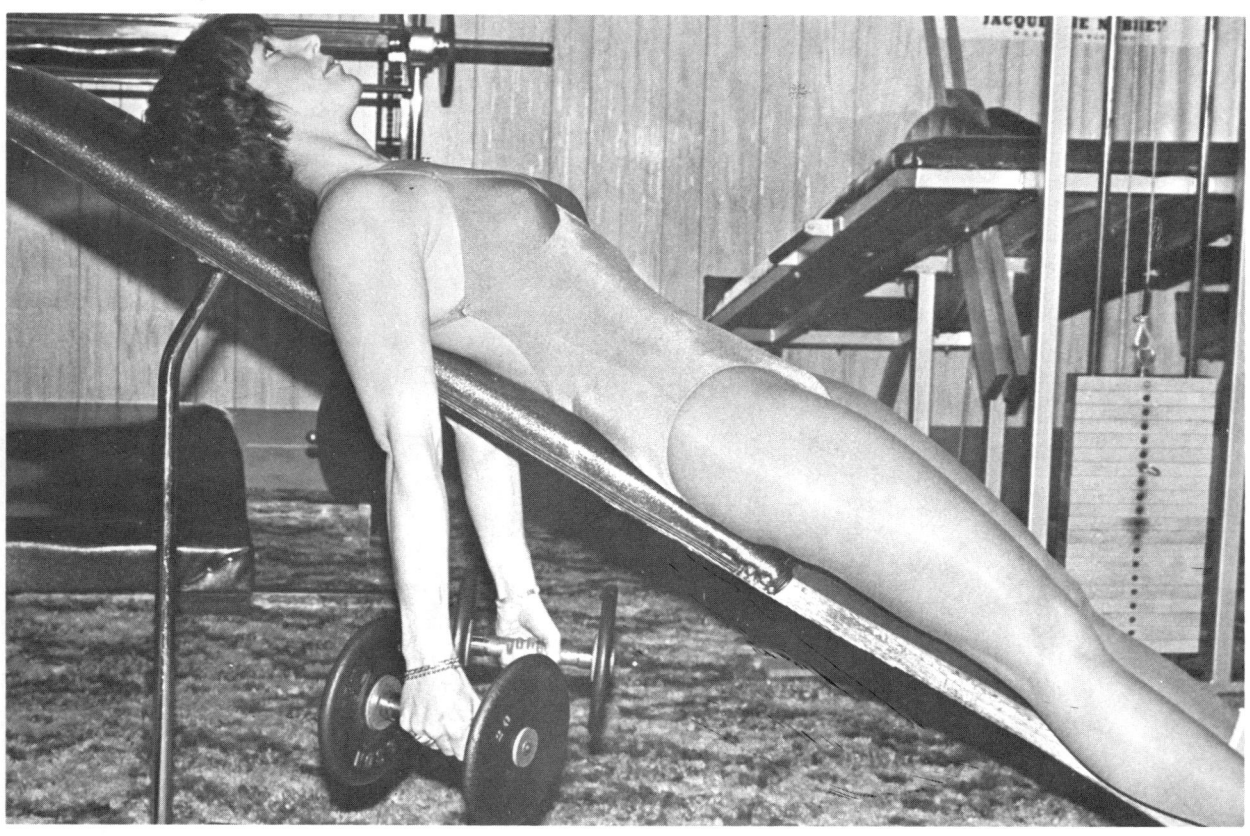

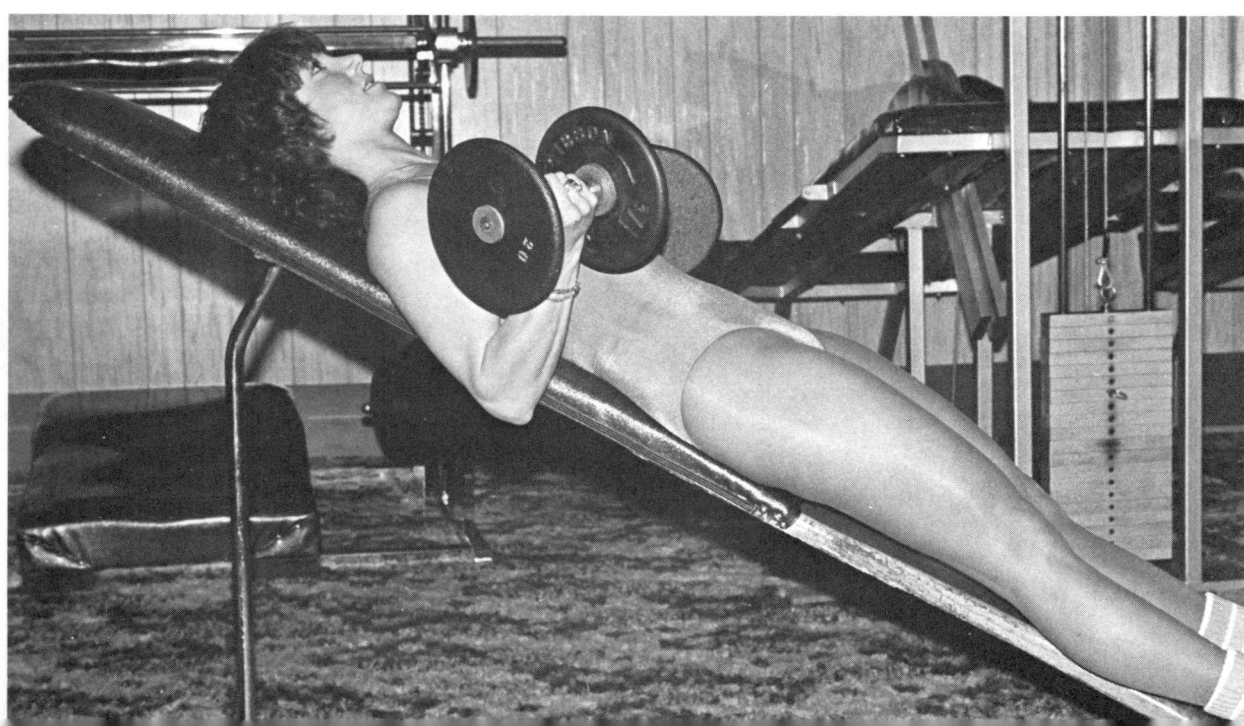

FOR THE THIGHS

Squats are great for the buttocks and the whole lower body. With a barbell held in position across your shoulders, head up and back straight, lower yourself till your thighs are parallel to the floor. From that point return to starting position. For some it might be useful to place a block under the heels as a means to maintaining balance. Breathe in as you squat and out as you recover.

FOR THE THIGHS

Leg press: Take up the position illustrated. Then press the weight with your leg strength until your legs are completely straight. Now let the weight down slowly. Make sure to keep the base of your spine and upper portion of your buttocks on the bench as you press in order to avoid strain to the lower back.

FOR THE THIGHS

Leg extensions (for the quadriceps). Check Lorie Johnston's position at the start of the movement. Hold tight to the sides of the bench, then straighten your legs until they are parallel with the floor. Hold the position for a count of two before lowering.

FOR THE THIGHS

Leg curls (for thigh biceps). Lie face down on a leg extension machine, as illustrated by Lorie Johnston here. Try to keep your hips flat on the surface of the bench. Now curl your legs from the full extension position, up as close to your buttocks as possible. Lower the weight slowly and repeat.

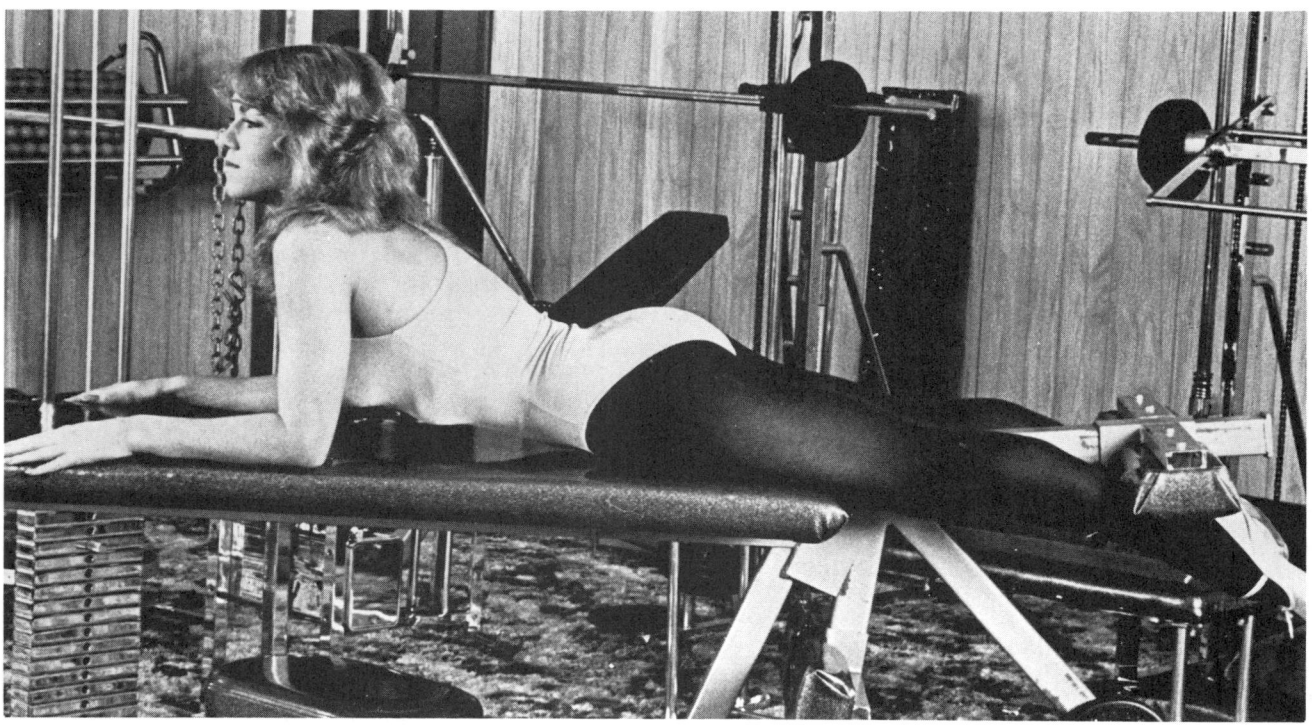

FOR THE THIGHS

Lunges (for hips and thighs). Stand erect, feet together, with a weight held as shown. Now take a step forward, bend the forward knee, at the same time lowering yourself until the other knee is less than an inch off the floor. Repeat with other leg. Foot position can be varied for different effects to thigh area. Experimentation will decide the best method for you.

FOR THE THIGHS

Deadlifts are great for the lower back, the back of the thighs and the buttocks. Stand with a barbell held as illustrated, your feet about a foot apart. Holding your back straight, bend down as far as you can go without allowing the barbell to touch the floor. At finish you should be standing erect. Breathe in as you go down and out on the recovery.

FOR THE THIGHS

Rear leg raises (for the buttocks and lower back). Take up the position shown by Lorie. Note how Lorie steadies herself by firmly gripping the sides of the bench with both hands. From the starting position raise the extended leg back and as high as you can. Keep the leg straight throughout the movement. Do 15 repetitions with one leg then change position to work with the other leg. The exercise is made more effective when done on the cable machine, as shown by Lorraine Snyder.

FOR THE THIGHS

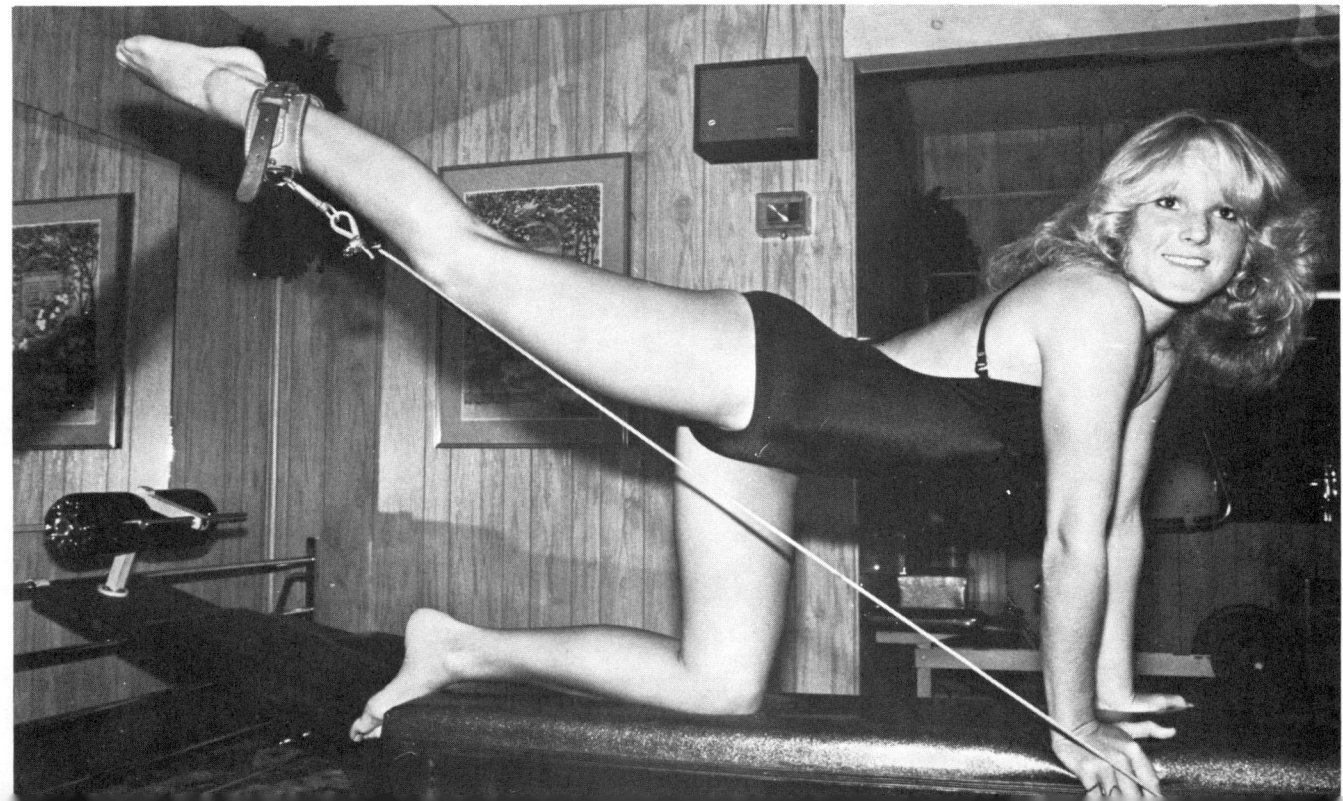

FOR THE THIGHS

Leg raises while lying on the side. This is great for the inner thighs and it also has good effect on the waistline. Take the position shown by Lorraine with the attachment around one ankle. Now lower that leg slowly, as low as you can go before bringing the leg up again. This position without the pulley attachment can be used to work the outer thighs.

FOR THE THIGHS

Inner and outer thigh machines can be used to work those areas very effectively. The machine on the left has resistance on the downward movement to work the inner thigh. The machine on the right works just the opposite so that the resistance is on the upward movement to work the outer thigh. Great exercises for those hard to work areas.

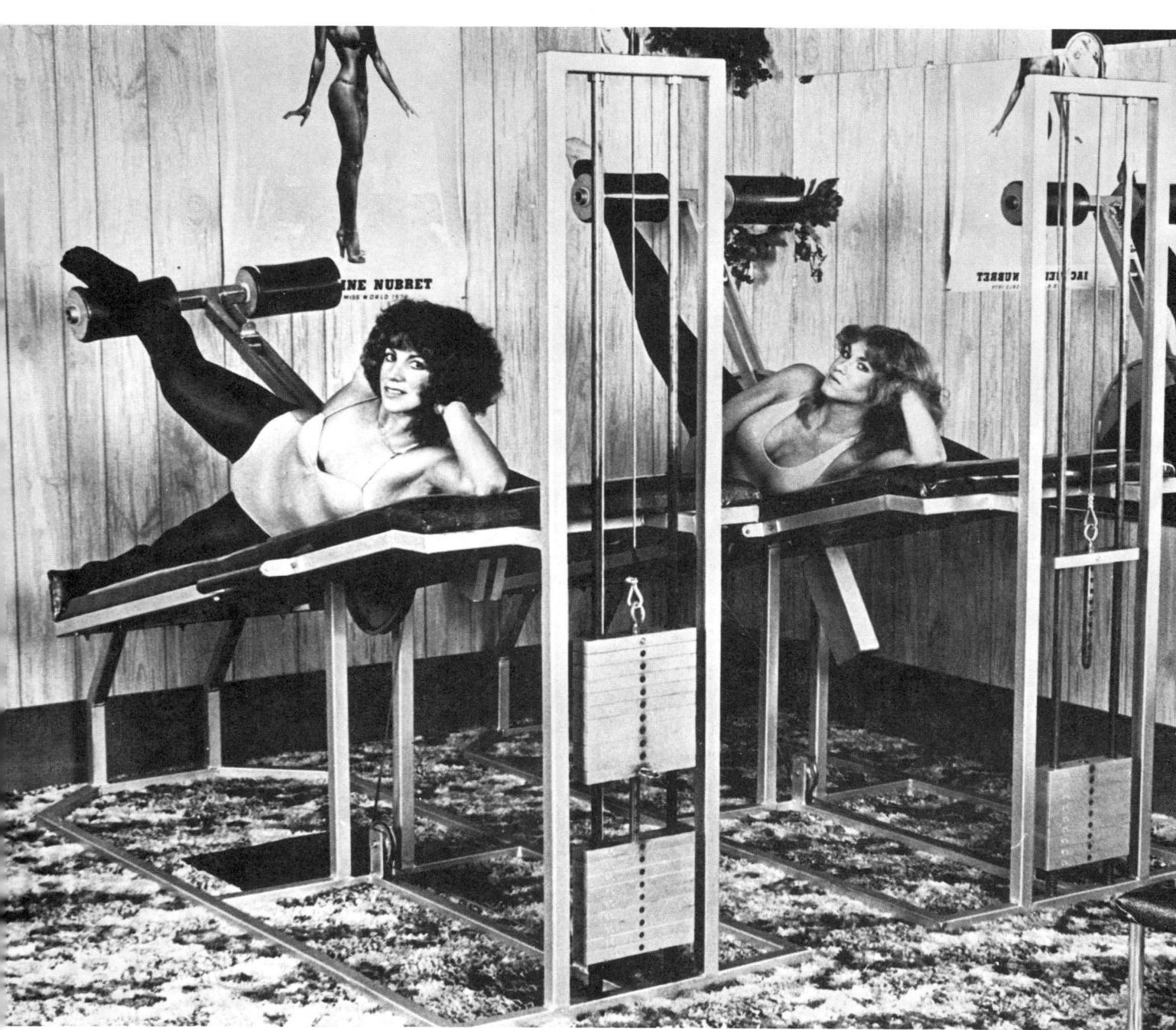

FOR THE THIGHS

Standing leg raises (for thighs and abdominals with resistance: Attach lat machine connection to one ankle, as illustrated by Lorraine and April. It is a good idea to hold onto a bar for support. With the ankle attachment in place, lift that leg straight and slowly in front of you, as high as possible before lowering to starting position. After about 10 to 15 reps place the attachment around the other ankle and repeat the exercise with this leg.

FOR THE THIGHS

Hacks: This is another version of the squat exercise and great for creating that long look in the thighs. Note starting position, feet apart, back leaning against the machine. Now breathe in deeply and lower yourself slowly to position shown. Return to starting position, pushing hard on your feet and placing all the stress on your thighs. Breathe out and repeat.

Photos courtesy of "Body Magic" by Lorraine Snyder. That's Robby Robinson, Mr. Universe, joining in the fun of the photo session.

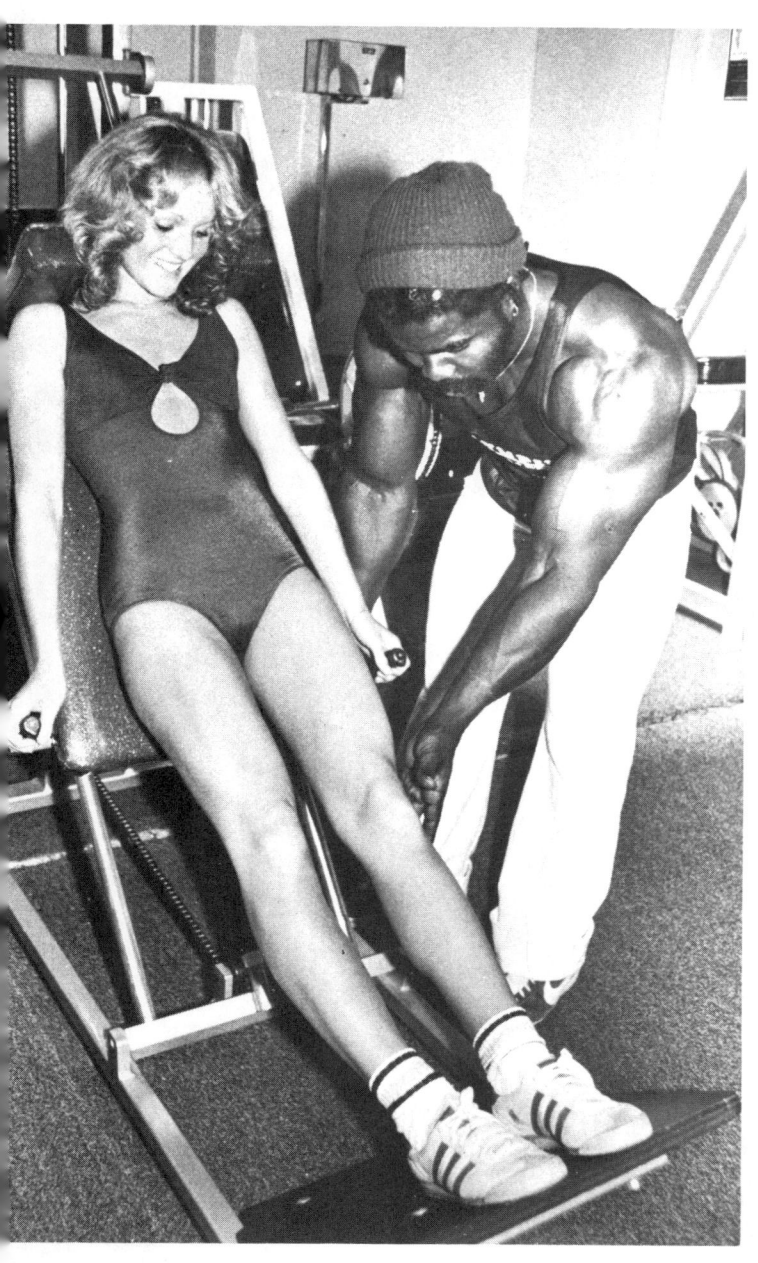

FOR THE CALVES

For the Calves: Heel raises can be done standing, sitting and lying on your back, as illustrated. Each variation has different, if subtle, effect on the calf muscles. The trick is to go up as high on your toes as possible then to stretch the muscles to their fullest by bringing your heels down as far as they will go. Development of the calves depends on this complete contraction (result of going up as high as you can) and full extension. With the standing toe raise, bend the knees slightly as you go up, then reach down with your heels as far as you can on the

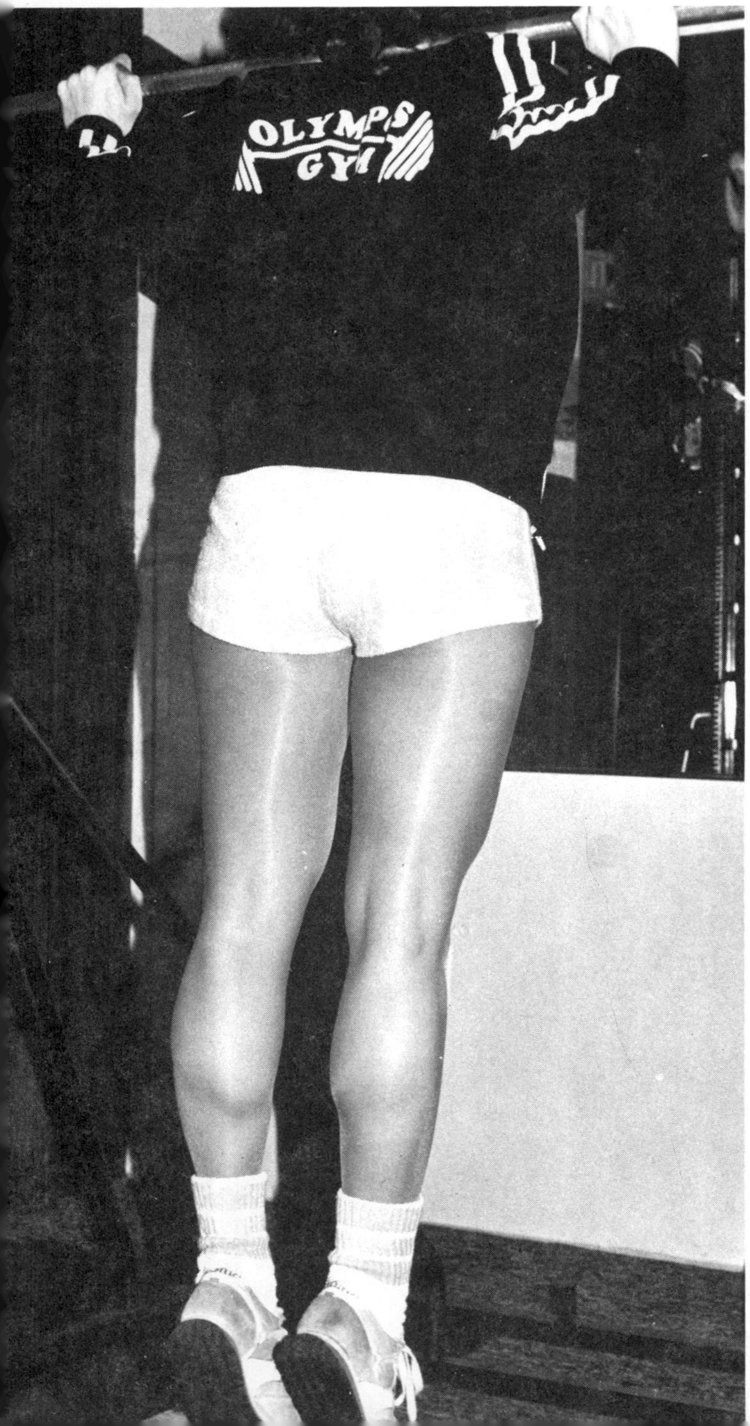

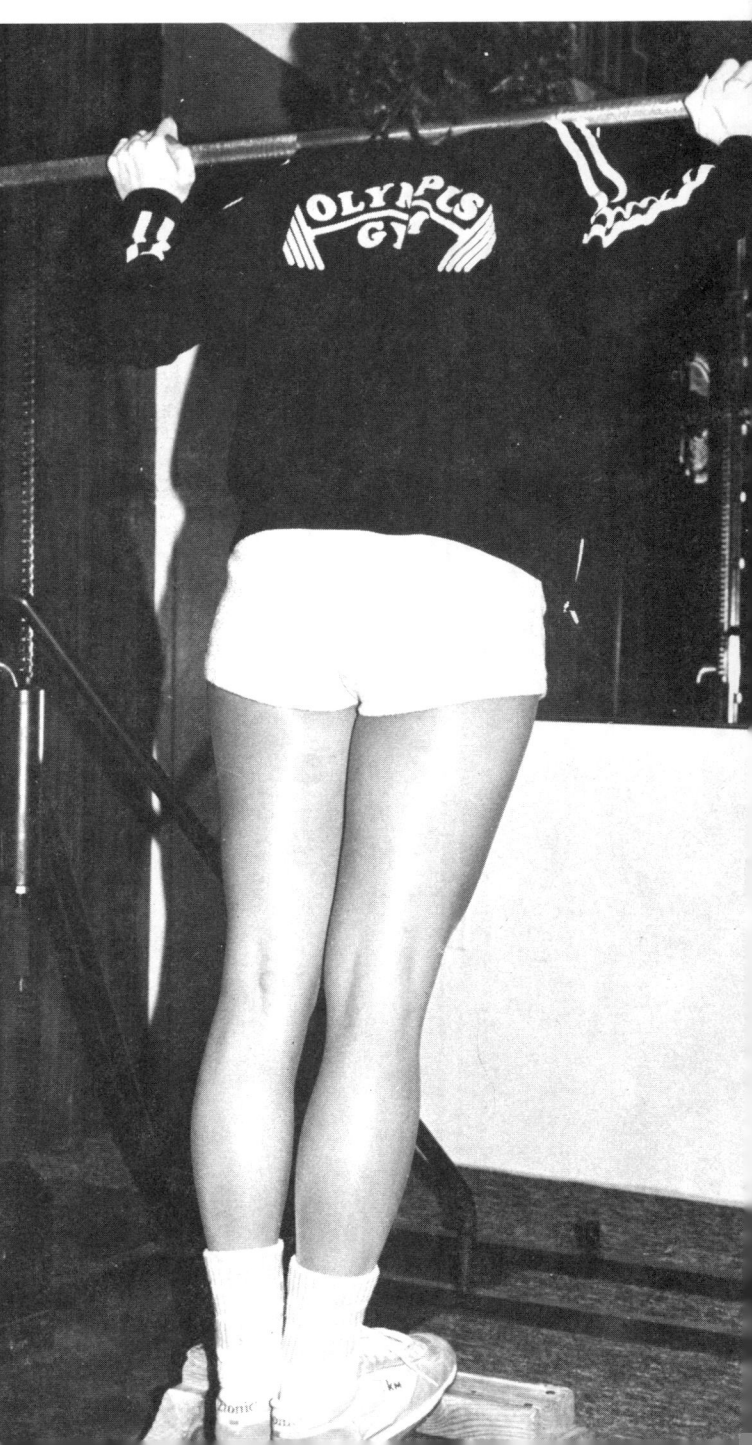

FOR THE CALVES

downward movement. The same principle applies when doing the exercise on the leg press machine. Push up with the toes as far as you can go, then slowly let your heels come up till you can stretch your calf no further. Do a slow and concentrated movement for the required number of repetitions. In the case of the seated heel raise, simply take up the position illustrated, then with the big toe side of the feet bearing most of the strain, raise your heels as high as you can. It is a good idea to hold the highest position for a count of two before going down again to rock bottom. Repeat.

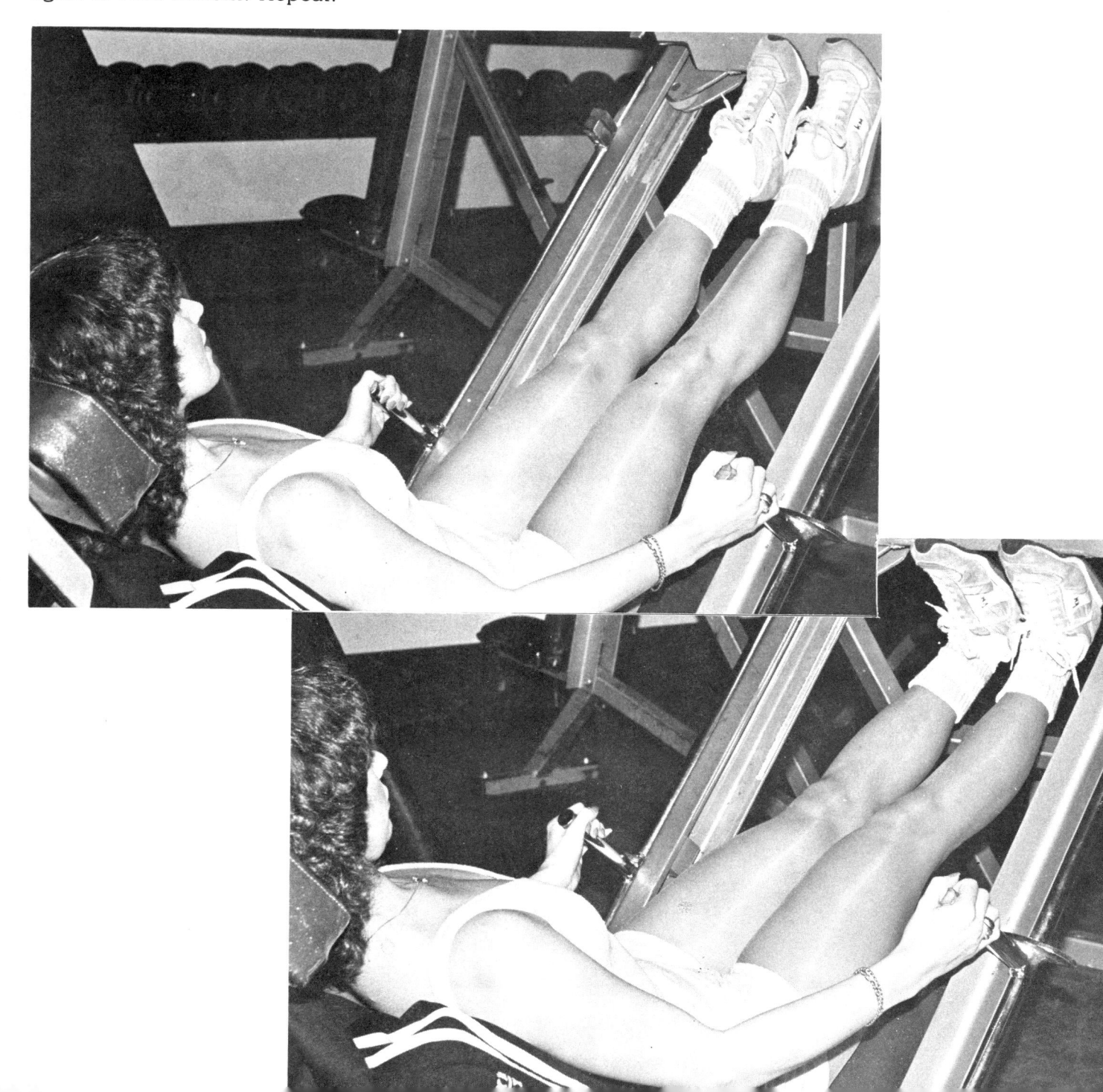

FOR THE CALVES

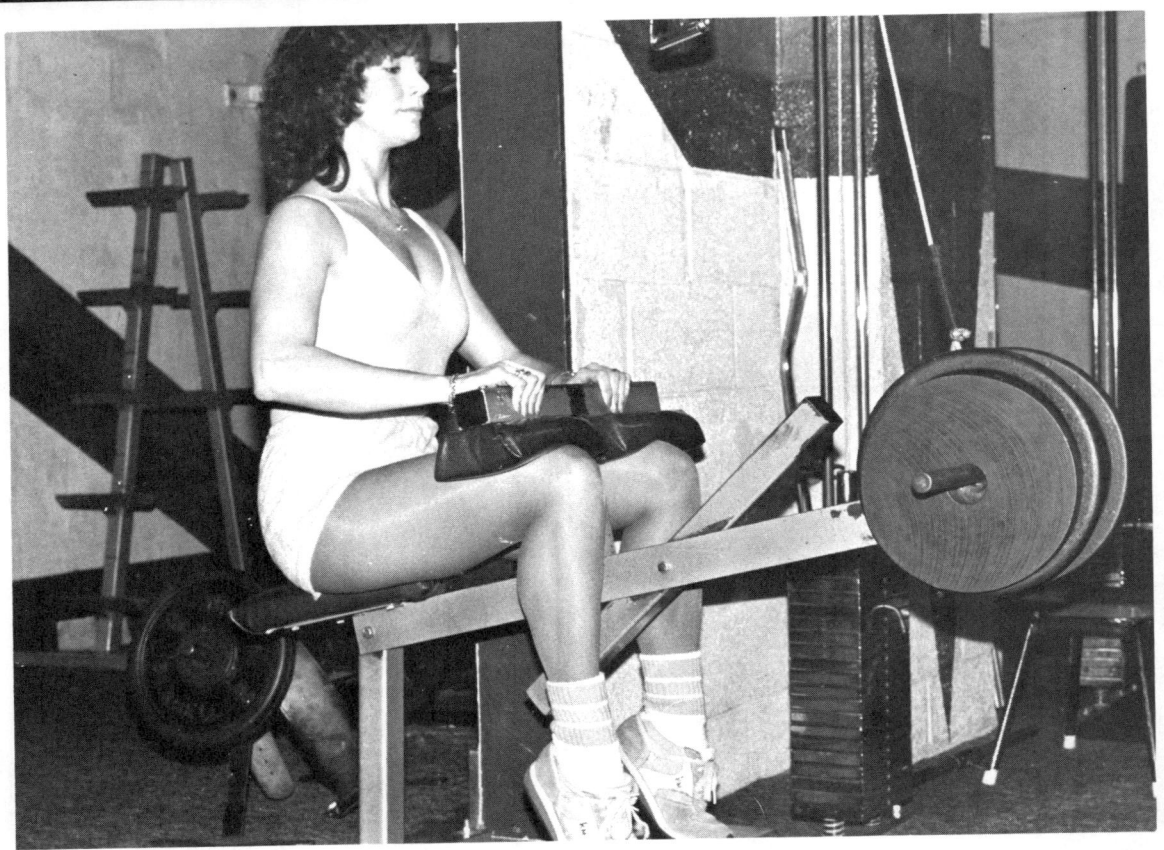

FOR THE WAIST

Roman Chair situps: Lorie Johnston illustrates the starting position. From there, breathe in, then lower your body backwards to the point shown. Return to starting position breathing out. It is a good idea to try to keep the abdominal muscles under constant tension by not bringing your body too far forward on completion of each repetition.

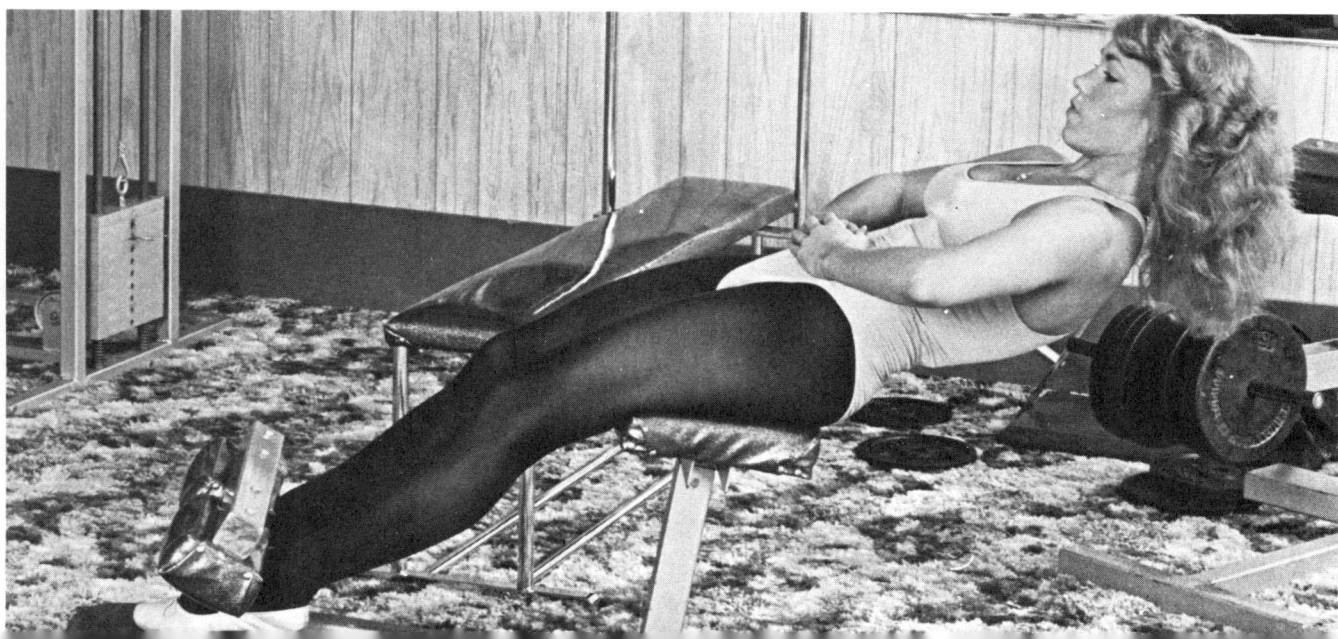

FOR THE WAIST

Decline situps. Adopt starting position shown, legs bent at the knees, feet firmly held down. Keep your hands at the back of your head. Now breathe in and slowly lower your body to the bench, deliberately placing tension on the abdominal muscles. As soon as your back has touched the bench start on your way up again. Breathe out as you come up. Practice will help your breathing in and out rhythm. In as you go down, out as you come up. Beginners can start with situps on the floor.

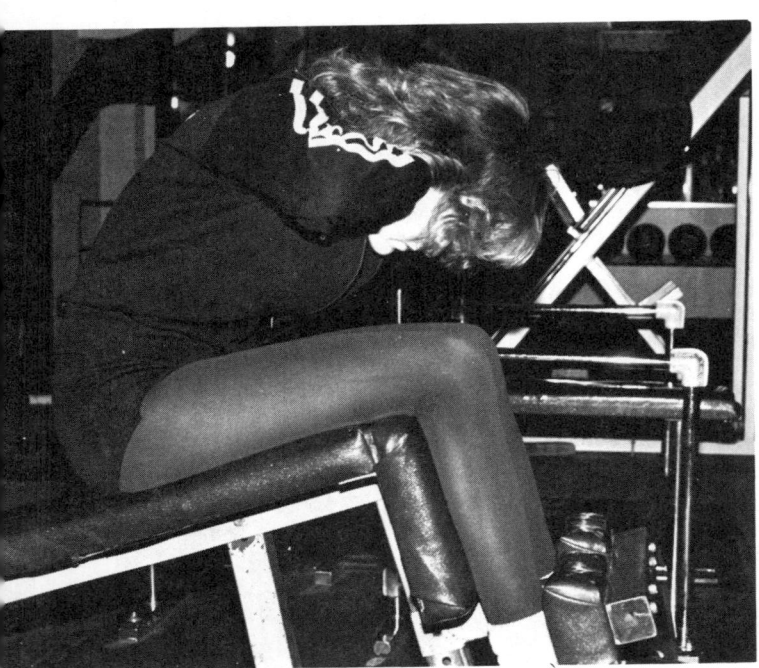
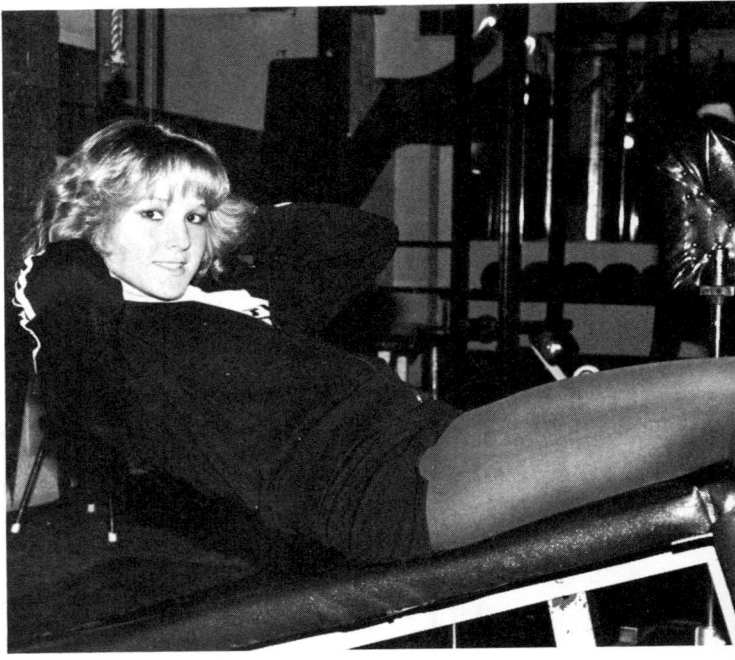

FOR THE WAIST

Knee raises are really wonderful for firming up the lower abdominals. The exercise can be done on an exercise bench as illustrated by April Nicotra or while hanging from a chinning bar. The principle is the same. Note that April is gripping the sides of her bench tightly to maintain balance, legs out straight. From that position breathe out, then bring both knees up towards the chest, as far as you can go. Try to place stress on your abdominals. Now thrust your legs out again, but slowly. Remember this is an abdominal exercise and you should feel the effect of the exercise in that area mainly. Breathe in as your legs go out. Try to bring the knees closer to your head with each repetition. If you choose to do the hanging version of this exercise, remember the breathing sequence is the same. Out as your knees come up towards your chest, in as you lower them. But do the movement with deep concentration, regardless of the variation.

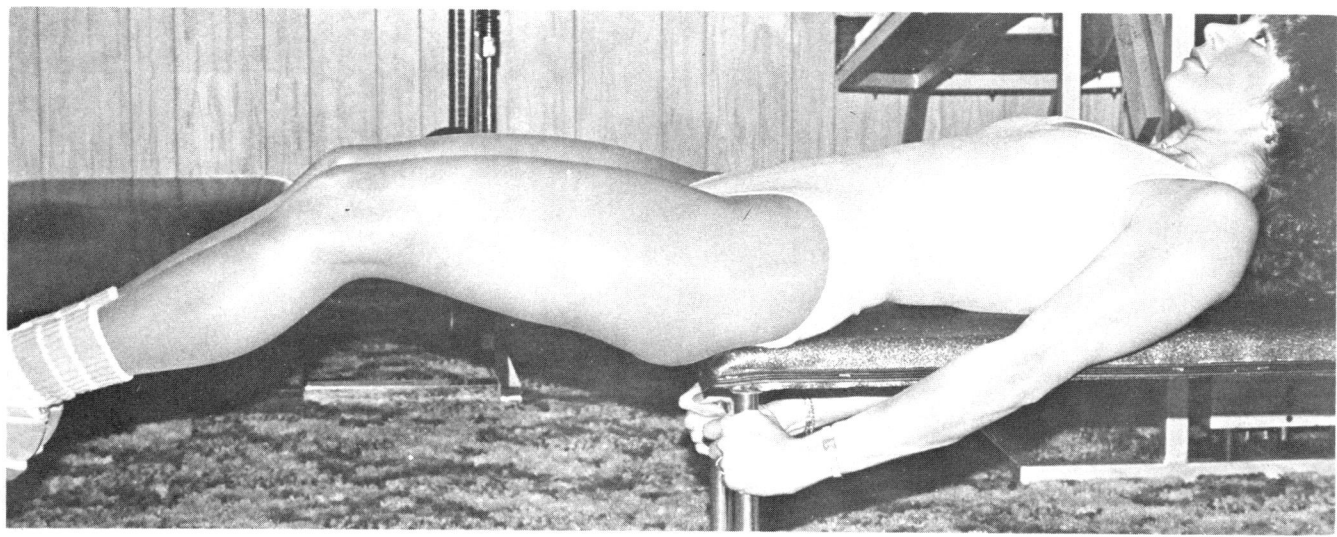

FOR THE WAIST

Leg raises: The starting position is the same as with the knee raise. From here, raise both legs towards your face as far as you can go. Lower again, breathing in as you do. The exercise can also be done while hanging from a chinning bar. Bend the knees slightly as your legs come up.

FOR THE WAIST

Twists work the fat off your waist and buttocks. The exercise can be done with a light pole across your shoulders or you may prefer to use the body twister. Both variations are shown here. If you are using the pole version be sure to keep your lower body as steady and to the front as possible when you vigorously twist your shoulders right and left. Be sure to turn as far as possible each twist. If you are using the body twister apparatus, then steady your upper body by holding onto a support, as Lorie is doing here, as you twist your lower body to the right and left. This exercise calls for high repetitions. It is suggested that you time yourself rather than count reps. Give yourself two minutes each set. Train vigorously, remember.

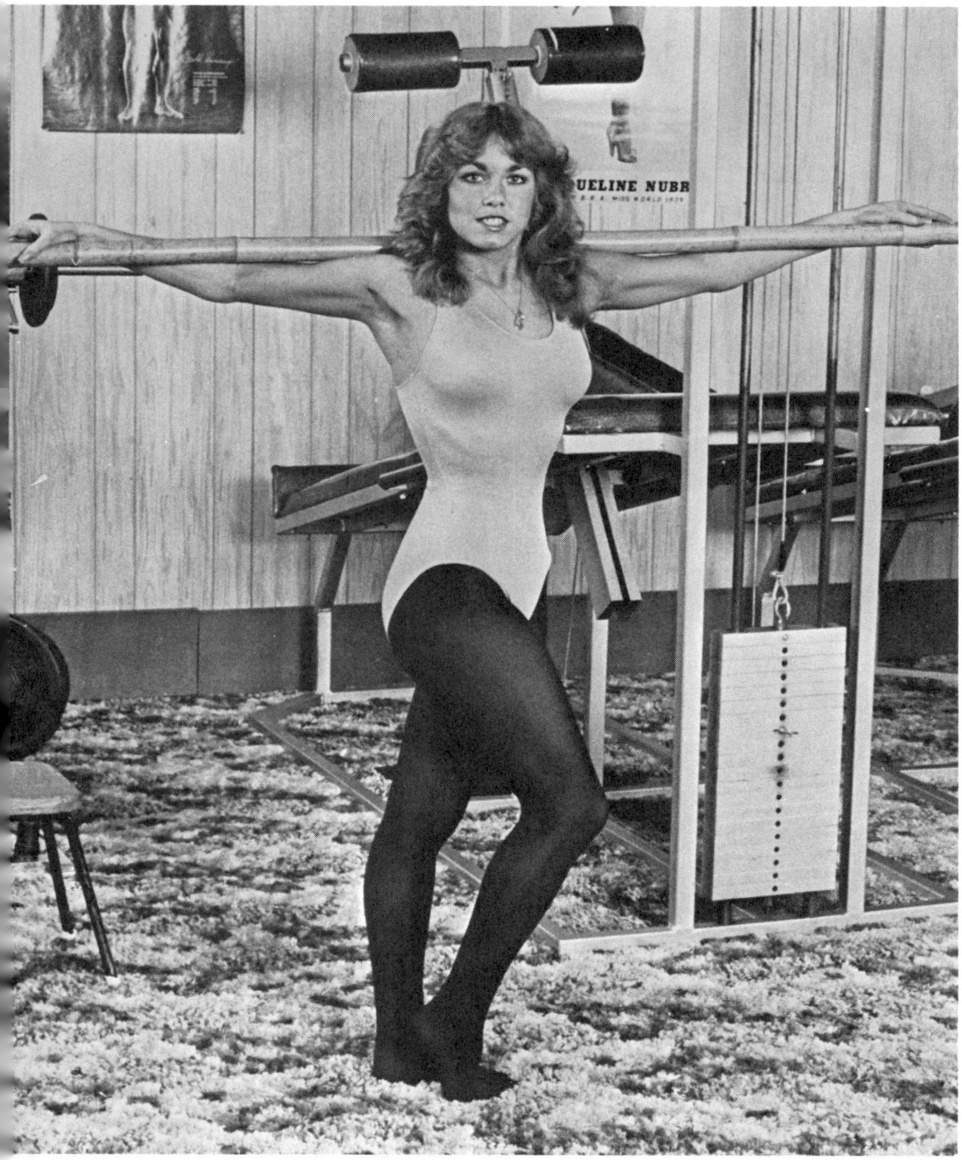

George Snyder owns and operates the Olympus Gym in Warrington, Pennsylvania. He and Rick Wayne have been friends ever since the latter accepted George's invitation to hold a bodybuilding seminar at the Olympus. Rick and George would collaborate in producing a bodybuilding manual entitled *Three More Reps,* which led all told to a 3-book series of the same name. Early in 1980, having achieved a reputation for staging some of bodybuilding's most talked about contests, George turned his attention to women's bodybuilding. He produced the much praised Miss Olympia, from which another book, *Women of the Olympia* has resulted. Naturally, Rick and George again collaborated on this latest work.